Later Selected Poems

Also by the Author:

Poetry:
Beware Falling Tortoises
Prisoners of Transience
Sing for the Taxman
Id's Hospit
Stonelight
The Beautiful Lie
The Movement of Bodies
Long-Haul Travellers
Selected Poems

Fiction:
Folk Music
Kirstie's Witnesses

Non-Fiction:
The Democratic Genre:
Fan fiction in a literary context

Later Selected Poems
Sheenagh Pugh

seren

Seren is the book imprint of
Poetry Wales Press Ltd.
57 Nolton Street, Bridgend, Wales, CF31 3AE
www.seren-books.com

The right of Sheenagh Pugh to be identified as
the author of this work has been asserted in accordance
with the Copyright, Designs and Patents Act, 1988

ISBN: 978-1-85411-497-6

A CIP record for this title is available from the British Library.

The publisher acknowledges the financial assistance
of the Welsh Books Council.

Cover image: The Lady Franklin Strait Party
© National Maritime Museum, Greenwich, London

Printed in Bembo by Akcent Media

Contents

from The Movement of Bodies (2005)

From *Sing for the Taxman*

Climbing Hermaness

Burrafirth

At the end of all things
there is a flower meadow,
a great meadow enamelled
with rose-root and red fescue,
a meadow of eyebright,
moonwort and tormentil,
a meadow of black cattle
wading through sunlight
and the scent of thyme, a meadow
with a salt edge, keen colours
blurring into shingle,
a meadow between two shoulders,
huge and green, hunched each side
along the glittering firth,
Saxa Vord and Hermaness,
shrugging at the Atlantic.

There is a great longing
to go no further, to be
beguiled, like the voyagers
of legend. *Why go west,*
the sweet whisper runs, *ahead
are dragons*, and someone leaves
the quest, to wander for ever
in the meadow of heart's ease.

But most go on,
shouldering their gear, looking
back at the jewelled grass,
because beyond the west
there is still a way westward,
because there is Hermaness
to climb, the last cliff
on the last island.

So they start upward, watched
by the incurious cattle
on the beach, munching blue gentians
that taste of salt.

Hermaness

The path is not, at first,
steep, more like a stroll
in the sun. When you look down,
the dust seems to glint; a child,
entranced, squats, pouring it
over his hair in handfuls.
The parents groan, but he rises,
holding both hands up, clean
and glittering.... There are gasps,
then explanations; gneiss,
silica, serpentine. Guidebook words
put things in their place. Ahead,
the child with the sparkling hair
touches a silvered finger
to his mouth, tasting the wonder.

The mountain sounds
with life: little peat burns
mutter underfoot, ribboning
the rock, grasshoppers whirr
like power-lines. The path
is mined with rabbit-holes
and black moths that start
out of the heather. A patch
of ground opens its eyes, gazes
gravely up, while the mother
circles overhead.

The climb so slow,
it is a small shock
to look down at black dots
browsing in the meadow.
There is mist ahead
where the mountain curves up
into a steep green wall.
Across the firth, the crest
of Saxa Vord is drowned
in whiteness; now and then,

when it swirls back, great domes
and towers appear briefly
and bright: the caliph's palace
of the air force, listening
from their outpost, scanning
the ocean for enemies.

It is a hut
on the edge of sight
you have to make for,
a smudge on the slope.
Sometimes the path, or the mist,
dips, and it isn't there;
when it comes back, it never
seems any nearer.

In the dips are patches
of bright treacherous green
that give underfoot,
sucking. The path stumbles
between heather-clumps; sometimes
an old plank wobbles
across quagmire. Either side
is the pale fluff of bog-cotton,
the sundew, that feeds
on flies, the spotted orchids,
just out of reach. *And do not,
on your quest, go aside
from the path*: all adventurers
get warned about that.

So long looking down,
picking the way; when at last
the ground firms, it is like freedom
to see the firth, the shining
sleeve pleated with ripples.
Look back: the meadow
is long gone, closed off
behind cliffs, their crevices
lit with sea-pink and the white
of kittiwakes.

The climb to the hut
is steep now, no path trodden;
too few come so far. The safe way
is marked with posts; you fix
the next in your eye. *I'll make it
that far.* The pure air rasps
in the throat: all adventurers
lean on that wall, as if
there were nothing left
to take them on.

Muckle Flugga

The marshland is left
behind, and the brown peat-burns.
You are higher here than snipe
or pipit, higher than butterwort
or yellow asphodel,
higher than water,
except the fine salt spray
that hangs in the air.
Colours are colder, squill
small and blue, like a haze
above the grass. Up here,
the fiddle-scrape of crickets
dies in the level note
of the wind. Even the clamour
from the raucous gannet-ledges
drifts up muted.

There is a coldness
of mist, sun-pierced; it swirls
below you, blanking out
the world. Somewhere down there
is the great sheet of brilliance,
the northern ocean, and the rock
of the last lighthouse.

It is not in the tale
that the adventurers come
so far, and cannot see it,
yet it could be. The chill
settles about; there is no reward
for climbing; mountains owe nothing.

But it does clear,
briefly; in a swift moment
it scrolls back, and you search
the blinding brightness for the black
of Muckle Flugga. And you see,
just for an instant, the tower
gleaming through rags of mist.
And beyond the last lighthouse
is the last rock,
the Out Stack, and beyond that
the resplendent sea. And when
the mist pours back, it is almost
welcome, in that place
of ultimates with no end
but light itself.

The old voyagers
would have set sail, hearts thudding,
for the edge, but you know
there are no edges.
You have outclimbed water and land,
you have come to this place
which is sky-coloured flowers
and salty grass, which is wind
aching in the ears, which is light
locked above whiteness,
and there is no insight, no knowledge
to take back: not the flowers,
nor the rare minerals, nor the black moths.
What lives here is for itself:
it must stay, when you go down
the only way you can.

Polar Bearings

An airport with a couple of runways,
a small terminal and a white bear.

He was spotted by a baggage-handler
last month, glimmering on the rim
of arctic dark; baggage-handlers go
about their work in twos these days.

In the transit lounge, people chat about him
offhand, glancing out of window
once in a while. Pilots take off
for the safety of meteor-showers, unwind
to the radio-static of ice-hail, flying blind
and relaxed over the Barents Sea.

Touching down again with a nervous laugh,
they hobnob with scientists, oilmen, a sightseer
or two. There's no such thing as a stranger
any more; they're all in the same story
in the airport on the edge of light,

seeing further, hearing a footfall,
hearts racing, living at the limit,
tasting the cold, the coffee, their own fears.

And when the fog sweeps in, piles in a drift
against windows, there's a communal
intake of breath. Who's to say, when it clears,
there won't be a patch of white left?

Book

I am the thought that flies in seconds
through a man's head, and lives for ever.
I am all he knew; I am his words
on the other side of the world,
sounding long after he dies.

I can change the world, build bridges,
change your mind, choke you with tears.
I can make a world, and man it.

Give me to a child, I am the ocean
cupped in his hands; I am all the sand
of the beach in his toy bucket.
I am the key to the walled garden,
the magic lamp, the island
where the treasure is.

I am could-be and might-have-been,
the story of the people, the store
of seed-corn. I feed the hunger
that grain leaves keen.

The Last Wolf In Scotland

I am a wolf. I know this
from way back, when my mother's
hot tongue prickled over the heap
that was me and the others,
as she whispered *wolf, wolf, wolf, wolf.*

There are four kinds: wolf,
not-wolf, wolf-food and hurt-wolf.
Not-wolf does nothing to the world.
Wolf-food is warm, floods your throat,
fills your guts with sleep. Hurt-wolf
stiffens hairs, sharpens eyes and ears,
thumps inside you.

         Wolf smelled different
from the world. When I was young.
all the dark smelled of wolf; later
we blinked our way into a dazzle
of smells, a music, note overlaying
note, but always the deep one
under all.

         The other day
I went to drink, and wolf
looked up at me. I'd forgotten
the face. So long since I touched
wolf. I used to find
tracks sometimes, or fancy I heard
a call at full moon. Never near.

I miss that smell, the gap
in the pattern, the note I can't hear
in the music. I miss fur and tongues
and singing voices. I miss the piece
that fell out of the world.

The Slow Fall

It was the first frost of October,
the first morning with enough chill
to chip the leaves. They wrinkled the canal
like a golden skin; you could see no water,

and the black barge came on slowly,
scissoring the cloth with its bow,
but in its wake was still seamless yellow,
as if nothing had ever been by,

and the stave's bright notes fell through the sun
like ash or dust. One glittering coin lit
on the steersman's hand; he smiled and waved it
in passing at the still, grave fishermen.

Five Voices

1. Johann Joachim Quantz, flautist

I met the late Lieutenant quite often
in the Prince's rooms. I shóuld explain
that the King's Majesty never approved
of his son learning the flute. Lieutenant Katte
used to keep watch and give us good warning
of his approach. It didn't always work.
I remember one time, he leaned
round the door. "The ogre's coming
on the run. I'd lose that fancy gown,
if I were you." This was an over-robe
the Prince had on; he threw it in a corner
and we all started stuffing sheet music
down the backs of sofas. The Lieutenant
couldn't stop laughing; I felt sick
with panic. He gestured at my coat.
"You know red puts him in a bad mood?"
We could hear the King's voice now, bellowing
along the corridor, and the Prince
was chalk-white: "Katte, he'll smash the flutes."
The Lieutenant clapped him on the shoulder,
(I could never get used to his lack
of formality, his casual manners).
"It's all right, we'll hide 'em." He grinned
at me, and opened the big wood-cupboard
– half-empty, thank God. I huddled with him
 in the stuffy, resinous dark, door held shut,
listening to the bedlam. Mostly shouts
or thuds, as the King fetched some book a kick;
once there was a great crackling sound
and an odd smell. The Lieutenant nudged me
and whispered, "He's pitched the dressing-gown
on the fire." His eyes gleamed. I swear

he enjoyed the danger. I was rigid,
my palms hurting where the nails dug in,
I only hope he doesn't look in here.
Catch me in a red coat again,
or passing the time of day with princes
and mad officers who can't stifle
inapt mirth... He was still convulsed;
my hand itched to hold his mouth shut
(is that etiquette, in a wood-cupboard?)
It seemed an age before the door slammed
behind the King, and we stumbled out.
I had cramp in both feet; he was still laughing,
until he saw blood on the Prince's mouth.
That sobered him cold enough; his face froze
like a hard winter. Myself, I took my flute
and my departure. I'd had enough
of the quality. If I think of him now,
he's always laughing in the dark.

2. Peter Keith, ex-Prussian Army officer

Damn beer's flat. A man might as well
be in the army. God, I don't miss that.
I never had any dreams of glory,
but in Prussia a man had no choice;
the whole bloody country was a barracks.
I was born to it too, but... I don't know,
my people weren't native Prussians, you see,
just Scottish adventurers who'd fetched up
in foreign parts. I've never felt at home
anywhere, so the idea of exile
didn't worry me, not that I ever thought
it would come to that. Well, would you credit
a crown prince planning to skip the country?

Oh, he had good cause, no question.
I was his best friend, bar his sister
and Katte, and never a day went by
that he wasn't shouted at in public,
kicked round the carpet, mocked, whatever
took the old goat's fancy. I'd not have stayed
at home for that, but then my father
wasn't the king. *Nobody* walks out
on a kingdom. When he asked me and Katte
to plan it for him, I really thought
it was just a dream; it'd keep his spirits up
maybe, but come the day, he'd think again.
I didn't do much; arranged a few horses.
It was Katte with his class, his gift
of the gab, who spoke to the embassies,
squared the French. And I never thought
he meant it, either. I mean to say,
he *was* army, a field-marshal's grandson,
for all his books and music. Besides which,
he never sounded serious about anything
for long. I've heard him spend half an hour
proving God didn't exist; he'd have talked
the Pope round. So I asked, since when

were you an atheist, and he grinned,
"Since it got fashionable."
It was one day
I went to his rooms, I think, to borrow money,
and I stopped outside because I could hear
a woman: the usual, I thought,
but it wasn't. This was a lady, speaking French,
arguing with him, and I knew the voice.
"It will never work; you must talk Friedrich
out of it", and it came to me then;
it was the princess. She was very angry;
Katte was trying to laugh it off,
and they say she was sweet on him, you know.
"If you think a prince's friend walks safe,
you're wrong." Then him, stung for once:
"If I die, it will be in a good cause."

Die? I damn near did. I sat on the step.
God, he's right, we could, it's desertion,
treason, what have you... My mind was whirling:
it was happening, the fools were going through
with it, and I wanted out. *She* knew,
who else? The old bastard had spies
all over the household. Good cause, be damned:
if I die, there'll be nothing good about it.
I'd have run that night, but I was too scared
to make my mind up. I hung around
a few days, biting my nails, till someone
tipped us the wink that it was all up,
and I rode straight for the border.
Why Katte didn't,
I can't think; maybe there was some girl
he had to say goodbye to, or maybe
dying in his good cause appealed to him.
He did it well, from what I heard. Here's to him.
This beer isn't as bad as I thought;
I must be getting used to it.

3. Georg Lisiewsky, portrait painter

I know that head. I've had the brow
in my calipers; I know the exact span.
I know how the eyelids half-close
in mockery, I know which colours to mix
for the pale tint of the hair, I know
just how much to darken it for the lashes.
There's a grin that starts at one corner
of the mouth, and when he speaks,
the head tilts slightly back on the neck.

On the neck... dear God, how long
are they going to leave it there uncovered?
I have never seen anything so wrong
as that head lying alone, apart
from the slumped body, arms flung out
at odd angles, and nothing as it should be.
I couldn't get the arms right; three times
I painted them over, and the natural line
still wouldn't flow, under that uniform.
It worried me; him too. I recall
our first sitting. "I want it done soon,
and done right." He was easy-going
in most ways, but he said that
in dead earnest. I wondered why
so urgent, such a young man as he was,
with all the time in the world.
                              The day I told him
I had the face finished, he came round
and looked a long, long time. He nodded
in the end. "Yes, it's good, it's like."
That was praise, from him, though he seemed
quiet rather than pleased. He stood still,
just looking. "I'll be young a long time,
thanks to you. But the arms are still wrong."

It was next day, out walking
in town, I heard he'd been arrested.
Treason, desertion, I don't know. I thought,
what'll happen to him, and then,
if he dies, who'll buy the picture?
I followed the trial, the sentence, waiting
for a reprieve. One day, I heard
two officers talking. "He was warned, you know,
the day of the arrest; he should have been
long gone, but the fool hung around."
"Some girl, was it?"

                        I nearly said, "no,
he just wanted to see the arms put right."
But I don't know that. And now they come
with a cloak, a deep splash of blue,
and drop it over the awkward wreck
of limbs, over the fair hair tied back,
and I'm not the man with the skill
to put him right now.

4. Colonel Reichmann,
commanding at Küstrin Gaol

I beg to report that the execution
of Freiherr Hans Hermann von Katte,
formerly lieutenant, was carried out
yesterday, November sixth, according to orders
at Küstrin. As His Majesty wished,
the Crown Prince witnessed the event
from his cell window. Indeed, as the prisoner
was escorted to the block, His Highness
called out to him: "Katte, pardonnez-moi".
The prisoner replied, also in French,
that there was no need, and that death
would be no trouble. He then walked on
with the guard, exchanging pleasantries
as if nothing were amiss. He was quite calm
throughout the execution, which proceeded
without a hitch.
 As had been ordered,
the body was left, uncovered, for some hours
on view, before the family were permitted
to remove it. The prison guards inform me
that the Crown Prince fainted three times
in the course of the afternoon. All has been done
exactly according to His Majesty's wishes.

5. Theodor Fontane, novelist

It was a chill day. We waited, huddled
and stamping, outside the big house,
while the servant hunted up the key.
He took us over the road, around the back
of the church, through long wet grass
to a small, squat, red-brick building.
There was nothing romantic about it,
no following a light down dark steps
into a crypt; he just unlocked the door
and there they were, the carved stone tombs,
cold and ornate. He pointed them out
to us: the general, the field-marshal,
knowing which one we'd come for.

You must look in the corner for the bad boy
in his plain wooden coffin. He has been
on his own ever since he came back
by night, unannounced, without ceremony,
to be hushed up. Yet, ever since,
visitors have come calling on him
at the back of beyond. They take relics,
if they aren't watched; all the teeth
are gone, and the vertebra from his neck
that bore the sword-cut; some Englishman
made off with that, our guide told me
over his shoulder, keeping a sharp eye
on the white jumble of bones, the bright swathe
of hair still tied in its black ribbon.
I'd not have thought dead hair could gleam gold
like that: burnished armour, celandines
in March? I'll find a likeness later.

He was no great beauty though. I've seen
his portrait, done the year he died.
A face neither handsome nor ugly:
witty, a little arrogant, perhaps,
but very bright.

(Lieutenant Hans Hermann von Katte,
born 28 February 1704, executed 6 November 1730)

Remember, Remember

This slumped bag of rags in the barrow
isn't him, this sad clown's turniphead
not my tall soldier, my November hero,
my ruined sunlight. He has been dead

so long now: young, he fills my eyes,
but the children make him an old man
in their play, drag him begging for pennies
till fire twists his face and he dies again.

I saw his face when he died the first time,
the thin paper with the bones' motif
traced through it. There was nothing of him:
he swayed on the scaffold like a leaf

in autumn. Now the day of thanksgiving
for his death blows the boys out of school,
scatters their laughter. And the birds are leaving:
the wind tosses them in a white handful

at the heavy sky. Trees against the dark
burn: there's a young beech, leaves just kindled
gold at the edges, but the big oak
blazes yellow, and the rowan's red

crackles and glows. The old man who stands
in the wind's stream, letting the shreds of light
fly around him, might be warming his hands
at the fire, before the year goes out.

But the boys stacking their wood so high
don't guess that death will have to do with them.
When they start the blaze, it will go quickly;
a few hours to feast their eyes on flame,

before the white ash settles and the man
of rags, the sacrifice, topples and dies.
My soldier once told me the world would burn
before we parted, but it was otherwise:

it burns each year, and never licks the fringe
of the dark in me, growing like the fir
that is always black out, that does not change
for autumn's light, nor the white sky of winter.

Allegiance

The skill is leaching from his hands, moment
by moment, like light through the loose weft
of an afternoon. The burnish of talent
and success, the bronze that sun left
on his taut skin is dulling, as if it were
winter with him, but it is not winter.

He is glad now of small success,
where once the best would leave him hungry.
It looked easy, but it never was:
even with skill, the shots don't come easy.
They have not come now for a long time,
and it is growing harder to see in him

what once was: is, on the odd occasion
when the grace strays across him like sunlight
over an autumn garden. But what's gone
is gone; these late rays can't kindle it.
Goodbye the fun, goodbye the fearlessness
and the endearing certainty of success

that comes of being young, and no intimate
of failure: they're on better terms now.
He has so much practice in defeat,
its gracious words, its gestures: few know how
to manage it as well. A master
of defeat, a specialist in failure.

And I would give brighter prospects a miss
to walk in the bleached leafless garden
with its sudden gleam of berries, its trees,
black and arched, its late roses half-open,
brittle with frost. It is easy to follow,
the memory of its paths, under snow.

The Silver Kite

Coming back from Kwik-Save, kicking litter down the street
where the crazy woman in her dandelion garden
curses all comers in a monotone, he sees
the silver kite. The sky is flat blue, the glint
so high, he takes it for a jet, but it flutters
and swoops, no bigger than a scrap of tinfoil, sunlight
flashing morse off it. His mind takes off, streams out
on the wind. He misses his turning, neck cricked,
following. It dances ahead, teasing him through
that grid of shabby terraces: one with caged saplings,
vandalised already, one with black bin-bags out front,
one like another. A man could lose himself
in sameness. He rubs his neck, eyes fixed on the glitter
in the air. There was a woman once, who passed him
with an echo of scent, and he tracked the bright wake
of her hair across town, to where he'd never been.
There are familiar routes; a man's mind is printed
like a rat's in a maze. The roads that lead to work,
to the hypermarket, to the petrol station.
He is starting to feel lost; he aches with looking.
It will hurt to turn his back, to let it go,
but he is such a man. There will be something wrong
with the job in the advert, the daydreamed adventure;
the girl with her kindling hair will turn on him
a plain face, and if he should find the silver kite,
it would be brash, tawdry. So he tells himself
as he walks away, his back to the light, denying
with every step the lift, the difference in the heart.

From *Id's Hospit*

What If This Road

What if this road, that has held no surprises
these many years, decided not to go
home after all; what if it could turn
left or right with no more ado
than a kite-tail? What if its tarry skin
were like a long, supple bolt of cloth,
that is shaken and rolled out, and takes
a new shape from the contours beneath?
And if it chose to lay itself down
in a new way; around a blind corner,
across hills you must climb without knowing
what's on the other side; who would not hanker
to be going, at all risks? Who wants to know
a story's end, or where a road will go?

Sandman

Cloud has scrolled over again, and a cold wind
blows seals into the bay, black brows gleaming
on a gunmetal sea, and there is no-one left
on the beach except me and the naked man

lying face down in the sand. He is growing paler
as he dries out; small silent grains are sliding
down the slopes of him, filling the hollow
of his back. Four sets of footprints head away

from the body: his and his wife's going straight ahead,
and a circling turmoil from the boy and girl
too old for sandcastles, who took such trouble
sculpting their murder victim. They were laughing

all the time, and the patient father, stretched out
on the beach to be posed and measured, was laughing too,
shaking his head, complaining his sepia likeness
was too short, building up muscles of sand.

His wife sat watching the dead man take shape
under her children's hands. She kept trailing
her fingers through her hair; as it fell back,
the grey would catch the light. She never laughed

with the others; even the brief smile flitting
across her face went out whenever she glanced
from her husband to the body like his.
When the sky darkened, and they were going,

she wanted to know if the tide would take him,
and they said no, he was above the mark,
and she left, reassured. I watched her out of sight
an hour since, and his right hand has blurred

into a white hummock. Wind shivers over him,
evening him out; soon the little sand-crabs,
scribbling their hasty messages on silence,
won't even have to pause when they come on him.

Brief Lives

Papa Stour

An island huddles against the gale
like a hunched shoulder. Fleece, manes,
grass, tears: all streaming.

Trudging against it, eyes down,
fixed on the ground. It's moving,
flakes of ash scudding seawards

then, suddenly, lifted
on a gust, tossed high. They're moths,
hundreds, pale see-through scraps

of airmail. They can't cling
to grass or stone; everything loose is leaving.
They can't steer,

can't assert themselves on a sky
that's pure movement. The wind is full
of waste paper,

brief wordless messages,
fluttering out unread
over the Atlantic.

Under Way

As the ferry got under way, he looked out
from its stern, filling his eyes with the wall
by the quayside, where he and Cal and Lowrie
killed so much time, and the island's one poky shop,
and the house up the hill with saithe pegged out
on a clothes-line drying, and Anderson's cat
taking a stroll. As they cleared the mouth
of the harbour, someone waved from the hill,
and it might have been Cal, but he couldn't see
for sure, and he fixed his gaze on one window
in one of the whitewashed houses. The boat lifted
on a strong swell, plunged, flew again
with the spray stinging. A couple of tourists,
wide-eyed, were watching the gannets dive
on fish, as if it were something special,
and already the roads were gone; the island became
two low green hills with a gleam of white
in the dip, where the houses were, just at the end
of the boat's wake. The mainland was edging nearer
behind a haze, sunlight drizzled through cloud,
but the island's micro-climate shone
under a bell-jar of blue glassy sky.
Sometimes it nearly vanished in a band of light
on the horizon, but if he screwed his eyes,
crusted with salt, he could still make a shape out,
and though the scattering wake no longer reached
so far, he could follow the line back
to the white gleam; it was still there, but only
because he knew it was.

Voices in Mousa Broch

Part 1: 1994

No-one lives on this island any more,
but all summer, all day when the ferry runs,
the tower is filled with languages, sibilant
Japanese whispers in the double walls,
Dutch gutturals echoing on the stone steps,
French, Danish, nasal New York, come to exclaim
into the steep height, admire its workmanship.

By nightfall they are scattered abroad again,
and the wall, that shammed so dumb all day,
comes alive, chattering, purring, hiccupping
in a reeking clamour of storm petrels,
its night-speech, its true summer language,
whose memory lasts it through the censorship
of snow, and the long monologue of wind.

Part 2: circa 1153

To Earl Harald in Orkney, greeting.
There has been no change. We are still outside
Mousa Broch, where we have been sitting
some weeks. In your last message, you suggested

we take it by storm. Have you ever seen
the place? It is a stone tower, quite round,
with walls a yard thick and one way in.
From its top, lookouts scan the whole island,

which boasts not a bush nor a tree for cover,
and God knows we could do with some, to dodge
the constant showers of arrows coming over.
They are well equipped, if I am any judge,

and well manned. The siege goes on, hampered
by the fact that we can find little to eat
in this bare place. The broch is stuffed with food;
he had it all planned out, I must admit.

We hear your mother singing, quite often;
she once climbed to the rampart, which we thought
remarkable at her age. The young man,
her lover, was there too, and in shot,

but they held hands, and we dared not chance
hitting her. She laughs a lot, these days,
and looks better. She shouted to me once
from the wall, "Tell my son I love this place".

If you were to ask me, I should say
that she was old enough to know her mind,
that I miss my bed, that my farm in Orkney
must be going to the dogs, and that this Erlend

of hers is one damn clever soldier
who would make a useful ally. The chill rain
has soaked into my bones, I shouldn't wonder.
I never want to see this place again.

Part 3: circa 909

I can't take my eyes off the fire.
I'm fixed here, staring into the flames,
listening for their soft flap and the sputter
when someone feeds them. They wrap themselves
round the dark. Eyes scorching, I can forget
Thorir Hroaldsson on the high seas
seeking my life.

Arnor is checking what stores were saved
from the wreck, seeing them stacked
in the rooms – rooms! Scrapes in the wall,
shadows seeping from the thick stone.
The girl in my arm shivers against me:
"They look like troll-holes".

Her mouth tastes cold and sweet.
Because of her, I am hunted.
I stroke her hair, thinking *I could die
for this*, and the blonde strands crackle
and burn my hand.

Arnor has posted sentries
on the wall's top, distant as stars.
He grins at me. "The little folk built
to keep out raiders. Odd, really;
would you think the poor bloody goblins
had anything worth taking?"

She burrows under my cloak,
her numbed fingers nuzzling
inside my shirt; my skin jumps.
Staring beyond the flames,
I see our shadows shift
on the wall; two dark folk
seeking shelter, like us and not like.

Part 4: ?

When you stoop in our doorways
you will feel we were small.
Measure our fear
by the wall's thickness.

The gulls that nest
each year where we lived
leave no less behind.
Our stone benches
took no impress.

In the shadows
of low-roofed cells
you guess at us,
around the bends
of narrow stairways.

But all you know
is the hollow in the millstone
and a white midden
of empty seashells.

The Fiddler Willie Hunter

1933–1994

An old man is playing the fiddle, perfectly,
slow as pouring honey, all his days
distilled into the notes. This is his tune,
a glass filling with light and white water
and sons a world away and ships sailing
and every fiddler on this windy island,
alive or dead, who ever made
a lament, and named it for a friend.

He has been dead a month, this man
who lives in the VCR, whose great gift
can be turned on when I choose to hear
his music. All that learning, all that grief
and joy turned off, as if the perfection
of a life's art were such a little thing
to the indifferent finger on the switch
that flicked him into blackness without thinking.

In his last weeks, racked with the sureness
of death coming, he spent day after day
in a basement room, laying down his music
on tape. He played without food, without rest,
till pain exhausted him; he would sit a moment,
then play again. They say he was never
so fired up, never put such loss
and passion into "Leaving Lerwick Harbour".

Last week a boy of fourteen, his pupil,
took first prize, playing a slow air
to the best judges, but behind his eyes
he was playing to his master... And there will always
be such another, the strings will always ring,
and a man be remembered in love
who has left a tune, or bent a boy's fingers
to the bow, though it is not enough,

nor the face on the screen that cannot be moved
any more by love, nor the twenty tunes he left,
nor the young pupils. There are still the other tunes
his mind never shaped, and all the pupils
who never knew him. Those he lived among
will keep him, because they were not done with him,
and would never have flicked the black switch,
being more generous than gods or time.

This Basement Room

This basement room. No sun gets in.
Its walls are soundproof. Outside
the air reeks of fish; a raucous scrum
of gulls goes down on the harbour scraps
and your wife's shoes clatter on the flags
as she hums your tunes. You wouldn't know.

The light slips by: six hours a day
in the northern winter. July nights
will be blue, uncertain, sun dawdling
on the sea's rim, no-one going to bed,
but you know you'll be dead by summer.
This basement room: hour after hour

you make music. The blank tapes fill with tunes,
tunes that waited, these many years,
while you ran the laundry, drove taxis.
fed your family. No Gauguin,
you were too good a man to be free.
The light slips by, but what is left,

all your life now, belongs to you
and your fiddle, and its loosed voice.
One bright morning, you feel guilty,
ask your wife if she'd like to go out,
spend time with you, and she answers,
"You make music; I'll bring food."

Your death coming set you free.
For all the pain, your bow-arm
flexes easy as ebb-tide
over the notes, easy as a man
coming home after years away.
All your life, you wanted this:

this basement room. The waiting tunes
belong to you, and all your life
fills the blank tapes. She brings you food
and sets you free. For all the pain
she hums your tunes. The light slips by.
Your death coming, you make music.

The Time Is Now

Never saw a sky so blue,
so keen a light, all summer long.
The time is now:
this month, this week, to walk among
the burning trees, till they snuff out.

In the great park there stands an elm,
yellower than sun in its chain-mail
of shivering flame.
The choir-school boys are playing ball,
team-kitted, shrill-voiced, making fun

behind Sir's back, or watching where
a girl swings past. The note of red
rings in her hair,
in rowan leaves, in the splashed blood
of berries, in the smouldering west.

The gates will shut before too long.
Late in the day, late in the year.
They look so young,
the girl with her bright fall of hair,
the boys in yellow, like the tree.

Two Retired Spymasters

They settled down beside the Suffolk coast,
in the flat lands where men can see for miles –
no hills to hide behind, no tricky forest –
They liked the villagers' polite, closed smiles,

the way a stranger always stayed a stranger.
They used to practise merging with the crowd
of tourists at the festival each summer,
just out of habit, just to show they could.

In the Cross Keys, trying to reminisce
without infringing Acts of Parliament,
they'd talk in hints, pauses, half-sentences.
And sometimes, by the window, they fell silent,

gazing out at the dark, the sundown sea
and the tired, sunken faces in the glass,
thinking how surely the last enemy
was edging up, for all their watchfulness.

Undercover

She walked toward me in a wall of glass,
so well disguised,
I swear, unless I knew, I'd not have guessed
the crows' feet on her face
were paint, nor that the grey came from a bottle.
It looked so natural.

At waist and wrist her bones were blurred with fat
slapped on like clay.
How did she do it? I saw her, quite lately,
walking as slim and straight
as any girl her age. She had them fooled;
she looked for all the world

like one gone forty; only I knew better.
Just an odd thing
betrayed her: that way she had of eyeing
young men… But then I knew her
so well. I couldn't see what others did,
and when I looked inside,

her eyes stared out, desperate and young.
I shook my head,
and she shook hers, and we almost collided.
I turned; she came along
beside me, mouthing *it's me; I'm undercover.*
I wouldn't look at her.

Captain Roberts Goes Looting

It's best when they surrender. No time wasted
on violence, just a few swift kicks
to the officers' groins, for luck, and straight on
to serious matters.

An ox-roar: Valentine Ashplant's voice,
he's found the rum. Young Bunce is slashing bales
of silk to bright shreds. And the captain strolls
to the great cabin,

pauses at the door, breathes in the musk
and sandalwood; these hidalgos do themselves well,
and there's the china. White, fluted eggshell
you can see through;

he strokes it gently. *We had some of this*
at Deseada; Val Ashplant smashed the last.
(He's bellowing again; found the sugar
to make rum-punch.)

Will Symson eyes a woman passenger
and meditates rape. But the captain has found
the tea, twisted up in papers. He crushes
a leaf, sniffs. Lapsang,

smoky-scented, and the next is Oolong
with its hint of peaches. Ashplant's delirious;
found the moidores that'll buy more sugar
and rum. Later,

back on their own sloop, the men cheer
the fire; they love watching a ship burn.
They've hauled over a hogshead of fine claret
to wash the deck;

it's like spilled blood, catching the fire's glint.
Captain Roberts sips peachy gold
from a translucent cup, wondering how long
it'll stay whole.

Captain Roberts Dresses For Battle

The gilt cheval glass has not been clean
since he took it from a French warship;
he peers through its clouds to the dull glow
of crimson damask. There's a long rip
in his breeches' arse, and an old gravy stain
on a sleeve whose lace cuff has gone yellow,
and he swears softly: *ach y fi*: a long way
from Casnewydd Bach to the Bight of Biafra.

There was a sycamore outside our cottage,
I used to climb it... What have I put
this sleeve in? He thinks back to when last
he stood before this glass: *was it the feast*
we gave that fort commander, Plunkett,
after he beat me in a cursing match,
Welsh against Irish.... when we lay
off Sierra Leone, six weeks of venery,

oh the black velvet.... He slips a cross
of fine diamonds on, and for a second
the face that stares out of the fogged glass
is the governor of Martinique
before they strung hemp round his neck
at the yard-arm. *My folk lived inland,*
that tree was like a maintop, but I'd sway
on the high boughs, hoping to glimpse the sea.

Cabin, glass, image shudder. *Grapeshot*
off the bow. How many crews have heard
my guns as close? The Sea King, the Fisher,
the Mercy, the Relief, small chance... I've boarded
four hundred ships since I was a pirate,
and I'm thirty-nine. The man-of-war's fire
jars the glass again. A swift glint of gray
in his black hair. *This damn glass is filthy.*

Now the pistols, on their silk sling,
and the sword. *This is the last venture,
one fight too many. And I will not go
to Corso, to hang a-sun-drying.*
He bows to the glass, his red hat-feather
brushing its likeness on the plain of shadow.
Then out. And jumps on a gun-carriage, as lightly
as a boy on a branch, and turns the warship's way.

Id's Hospit

I look out from a 17 bus:
more letters gone. ID'S HOSPIT
it says now, and one 'I' hangs loose.
The stone front is like a film set,

nothing behind, no wards, just a waste patch.
Sunday car boot sales. No profit in land
right now, Danka; it doesn't pay them much
to build there yet. A man turns half around,

looks at me oddly, and I know I spoke
aloud, spoke to you. I see you wave
from the window where I would look back
after visiting, not wanting to leave

you and Richard. You'd be holding him,
a white parcel; my son. I felt unreal,
dizzy with light. Never such a time.
Each night that week, the lads from the mill

took me out drinking. *Ryszard's got a boy,*
they'd tell the Taff Vale, the Panorama,
the Globe, the Greyhound and the red night sky
– a steel-town sky; you remember, Danka?

Not any more: years since I would see
a steel sunset. Jobs have got scarce
for the lads, and their lads. It's a harder city
than you knew, but there are places worse.

Under the high roads of Waterloo
– you won't believe, Danka – people have put
a town of boxes up. I saw a soup queue.
Old times come round again; who would have thought?

And who thought they'd sell the corridors
where you walked singing? The things I miss:
pubs have dress codes and names like Traders,
and I talk to myself too much these days.

Our saint has lost his head, and the healing word
is flaking off the wall, letter by letter,
and I can't recall behind which board
was her window. I suppose it doesn't matter,

and perhaps tomorrow I will go to London,
back to the poor shacks in the concrete shadow
and see if I cannot find my son
huddled in black, his face a boarded window.

Shore Lines

1. Redcoats

You know how it goes. The dark rock-face
in the mist is a warship, a pirate brig,
but she stands off, taking the shore women
for soldiers in their cloaks of red flannel.

It was the French, or John Paul Jones;
it happened on every coast in Europe,
perhaps. Or maybe the shape hardened
after all into a ship, maybe the blurs
at the rail turned to grins, avid eyes
that knew a woman when they saw one.

Those figures, stooped with seeding,
scrubbing, carrying, could they pass
for troopers? If they straightened,
kneading the ache from their backs,
if they shouldered their driftwood loads
like rifles, if they stood firm,
forcing themselves to look out
to where fear comes from?

Maybe it's even true that once
some young conscripts scrambled ashore
and surrendered to the first red cloak.
And she wide-eyed, watching a sea-wolf
turn up his scared boy's face.

2. The King of Sule Skerry

The woman with the black eye
limps under her creel to the tide's edge
where wrack fetches up, salty and fly-blown,
creaking underfoot. In freezing pools
she guddles for limpets to bait his line.
Out in the bay, a sleek head stands
proud of the water, shines at her.

It is the King of Sule Skerry;
she drinks the calm in the wide eyes
like water. Her hands starve
for his streamlined flanks, his soft
spun whiskers; she aches to lay
her cheek to his cool pelt.

Come ashore in a man's shape,
as you may do one night a year,
and I will hold you in a cave
and keep you from the cold white stars.

Then, with the sun, put on your skin
and take me with you on the sea,
and show me where you reign the king
of all the selkies on Sule Skerry.

He balances easy; she cannot swim.
Would you wait for me?
She has seen them beached, wounded,
flinching from the fishermen.
One held her eyes in a dark look
of hopeless complicity, as the club
came down. They cry real tears.

He says you tore his salmon-nets;
he made a fist of his red hand.
Away now, dark-eyes; don't wait.
My man will kill you, if he can.

3. The Monkey

It was not just Hartlepool,
oh no. I have come ashore
at so many ports, swung over
so many rails to stroll down
another quay.

I was always wearing
the jacket and little cap
my shipmates made me, always
smiling up at new folk.
And always

they'd peer down, eyes narrowing,
faces clouding over. I always
chattered reassuringly, forgetting
they would take it for French.
You shore folk

are not like sailors at all.
So closed, so edgy. Soon
the whispered questions would start.
"Is it a Frenchman?"
"I wouldn't know;

what do they look like?"
"He might be; they're little,
the mounseers." "That's foreign,
that jabber of his." "Better
be safe than sorry."

And there I'd hang again
for a spy, a stranger,
an outlandish tongue. Where I went ashore,
it always seemed to be wartime,
and folk were always on edge.

Jeopardy

FOUR HUNDRED JOBS IN JEOPARDY
– it had to be worth
taking a look. But often,
along the road, he was tempted to stop.

Across Cloudcuckooland, it was free sex
all the way, in Cockaigne
roast pigeons flew obligingly
into his mouth. He could have lain
all day by the lemonade springs
of the Rock Candy Mountain.

But he knew where he had to go.
Oh, the gingerbread houses
were fun, and earning a wage
for sleeping late, and winning
races by coming last. But he knew
Jeopardy was still the place.

And it was; it was better
than all of them. At the border
gates stood open, guards in deckchairs
glanced up to wave the refugees through.
A gleaming bus whizzed them
into the city, along wide avenues
shaded with palm trees, past parks
and playgrounds. He wandered clean streets,
shaking his head, gazing up
in awe at the crystal windows
of the great libraries. He breathed air
with no aftertaste, enrolled
in an evening class, found himself
a National Health dentist.

All night, he lay awake,
wide-eyed, knowing he'd travelled,
at last, out of the world.

The Woodcarver of Stendal

"Judas? You want Judas? Look,
nobody wants Judas." But the bishop's clerk
was businesslike, unbudging. "We've paid
for a full set of apostles, lad,
and we're 'avin' twelve."

Oh right, no trouble… The worst man of all time.
I stare at the harmless wood, trying to see him,
the abhorred face. How do you carve evil?
I knew I'd need more than one model
to do him from life.

Anger: veins throbbing on the thick neck
of Master Klaus, who didn't like my work.
The glint of coin in miller Martin's face
as he gives wrong weight. Liesl, drunk, shameless,
tugging my sleeve,

offering her blotched body… oh, my neighbours
were a great help, donating their coarse features
to my patchwork. I took the blemishes
of my kind, the worst in all of us,
to bring him alive.

But what happened then? He looks no sourer
than laughing Liesl, as honest as my old master,
who never paid me short, as sober a man
as Martin, who has eyes for no woman
but his plain wife.

Only a great sadness marks him out,
and that was mine. I scraped my heart
when I planed him. John, James, even Thomas,
they were names, nothing beside this Judas
noosed in my grief.

Frost Greyface

General Frost on patrol
goes the rounds of his territory
    — Nekrasov, "Frost Rednose"

This one does not come like a general,
bluff and booming, his tread shaking the night.
He sidles down the streets of the capital
soft-shod, soft-spoken, wearing a grey suit.

His hair is grey, and his expressionless face,
and greyness streams out of his fingers' ends,
silvering pavement cracks, misting the glass,
and silence grows, where he goes his rounds.

Frost Greyface is a fastidious fellow,
a conjuror; he likes to magic over
what's awkward and unsightly. Look now:
watch how he touches the huddle over there

in the doorway, and leaves it shimmering.
He hangs lace curtains to the cardboard shacks,
while on the black bin-bags, harshly wheezing,
you'd swear a thousand snails had left their tracks.

"Are you warm, lady?" Frost Greyface whispers
to an old woman about forty-one,
and she nods, and a sleepy smile wanders
on her blue lips, and she settles down

to stiffen like a white leaf on the tree.
Even the small smoke of her breath
on the air is unthreaded; she is nobody.
Frost Greyface laughs, leaps over her death

to make cobwebs glisten in the sun.
Now all the night's litter is swept away
and the city flashes like new-minted coin,
fit to dazzle the very eye of day.

The Frozen

Tackling that peak, the whisper says,
you may come across an Austrian woman
frozen upright, swaying slightly, her face
empty as the luminous snow plain,
a sky bleached of blue in her eyes.

She stands sentinel, but many sleep
where they lay down, starved in the bright air.
White contours shift, and they turn up,
briefly, like folk who look round the door,
wave an apology and can't stop.

And they say ships endlessly circle
where the Arctic drift-ice snapped shut.
They have been seen, the crews that cannot fall
to rest, locked into their last minute.
There must be a legion of these people:

brittle chrysalides, rustling hollow
wherever light distils and breath comes hard,
seeing over the edge and mouthing *no*,
rueful signposts on the one road
nobody ever yet wanted to go.

Ciphers

The tides erode a wader's precise prints
to a smudge, and the snail's silver signature
dries faint. So words keep the shape
of thought, of that vastness which absorbs
definition as easily as a blue sky
sucks up the calligraphy of smoke.

From *Stonelight*

Stonelight

Not the frailest thing in creation can ever be lost
– George Mackay Brown

Each stone happens
in its own way. One stands
true in a house-wall.

Anger quickens another: it flies,
fills a mouth with blood.

Shaped and polished, one shines
in the eyes of many.

One seems inert, earth-embedded;
underneath, colonies are teeming.

But the best are seal-smooth,
and the hand that chose them

sends them skimming, once, twice,
ten times over the ocean, to the edge

of sight, and whenever they brush the water's skin,
an instant is bruised

into brightness. The eye flinches. When they sink,
if they sink, the light they left

wells out, spills, seeds itself, prickling
like stars, on a field that never takes
the same shape twice.

The Arctic Chart

1. The Parry Islands

Winter man, first of your kind
to sail that great sound with its chain
of islands, scattering names

from home: Devon, Somerset,
Cornwallis, Melville. First to spend
long months of darkness

in an empty land. The snow
stretched so flat, distance
lost all meaning;

the eye strained for a mark.
You learned the word *cold*
in a new language:

the tongue locked fast
to a man's beard, the scald of metal
on flesh. Mercury swelled,

shattered thermometers. Steam froze
on the ovens. But you had looked
from a mountain, out over

the drifting distorted towers
shivering light
and sensed behind them

an immense mind, unexplored,
unbounded; you could never chart it,
though you knew its name.

Edward Parry, believer, searcher,
living in awe, more humbled
by each new wonder.

2. Fury Beach

On the barest of beaches, open to the gales
that drove her aground, they left her, all her crew
crammed in her sister-ship, looking back, anguished,
sick with the failure

of losing a ship. The luck had never been with them:
they had found nowhere, had nothing to show
for their journey north. Their captain was going home
to a court-martial

and *Fury* was lost, broken on the beach.
How could they know, defeat stinging their eyes,
her name would become a landmark for starving men?
How many stranded explorers

made for that beach where a ship's stores lay heaped,
food in the wasteland, boats to escape the ice;
how many saw through tears their lives given back;
how many men went home?

HMS *Fury*, built in Napoleon's time,
driven ashore by a gale on Somerset Island,
lost and then found, again and again: life-saver,
wrecked on a lucky day.

3. Kane Basin

Dead man running round the world, chasing
all the life you could get, one beat ahead
of your leaky, racing heart. Never pausing

at books or music: barely time to read
the world through your eyes, let alone another's.
A day without something new was wasted –

it might have been the last. The pretty manners
of your boyhood, left behind in your wake,
a comet's tail of casual hurts, sharp answers:

you weren't good at people. They take
too long; you'd other things to think about.
When you saw the winter ice break

with a great rippling wave, like a carpet
shaken out, when you heard the bergs grind
like rasping sugar, you were sensing it

with a rush of blood to every nerve-end.
Of all the drugs you'd studied, the most potent
was the world you'd have to leave behind

before you were old. Driven, impatient,
arrogant, all of that, and small wonder.
I doubt I could have stood you a moment,

Elisha Kent Kane, doctor, explorer,
poser, pain in the neck. My life has lasted
longer than yours already, and I will never
live half as much, dead man, as you did.

4. Bellot Strait

Little Bellot
they called you,
the home town
that paid your way
through college, the widow
you went to help
in another country,
who spoke of you
as her own son.

Wherever you travelled,
you saw brothers,
and so there were.
Your sledge crew wrapped
ox-hides around you
while you lay sleeping;
the Inuit, hardened
to kinfolk's death,
cried over yours.

You'd gone beyond
one land, one race,
calling all humans
your countrymen.
At ease among strangers
with a common cause,
you dreamed of nations
coming together
as men had done.

Joseph-René Bellot,
French officer, citizen of the world,
it was not your heart,
nor your unfenced soul
that caused a friend
to choose for you
the smallest strait
in the Arctic.

5. M'Clintock Channel

It grinds down from the Beaufort Sea, slow
as old men's jaws, a great stream of slabs
split off the ice-pack, rasping, crushing,
squeezing between the islands, Melville, Banks,
then down that wide channel east of Victoria,
a mile a month, and no ship gets past it

— none tried, for years. They'd see the ice-stream
and look for the way back. You looked
for a way round, a narrow, untried strait
whose icebound mouth drove you back six times,
a long, aching, sledge trek. You were a man
to do what you set out to,

a practical man, no dreamer. Yet you fixed
heraldic banners to your sleds, quested
at your own expense for the widow's husband,
refused her money, did what needed doing
as no-one else had. A man of deeds,
not words. Your words came slow

and plain: when you found the poor bones
bare in the snow, the abandoned luggage,
you hung no colours to your sentences.
They fell down and died as they walked along.
Leopold M'Clintock, prosaic knight-errant,
man of few words, every one exact.

6. Lady Franklin Bay

It lies in the north, lady,
where you never came,
in the white, locked world where you never
could follow him.

You went to the outer isles
at the country's end,
to ask all the homebound whalers
news of your husband.

As you came through the Davis Strait,
down from Baffin Bay,
did you hear nothing of my love,
who had passed that way?

You sent out your freelance captains,
Forsyth and Snow,
Inglefield, Kennedy, M'Clintock,
little Bellot,

to seek him, and every ship
took your thoughts with her.
The lie of that land, its ice,
its waters, its winter,

were all your study, as if
you could never know
enough of the place he was in
or what he went through.

Each channel, each strait on his way,
you could have charted.
– Oh lady, you were a widow
before your search started.

He lies in the north, lady,
where your heart came.
Nothing belongs up there
so much as your name.

Envying Owen Beattie

To have stood on the Arctic island
by the graves where Franklin's men
buried their shipmates: good enough.

To hack through the permafrost
to the coffin, its loving plaque
cut from a tin can: better.

And freeing the lid, seeing
the young sailor cocooned in ice,
asleep in his glass case.

Then melting it so gently, inch
by inch, a hundred years
and more falling away, all the distance

of death a soft hiss of steam
on the air, till at last they cupped
two feet, bare and perfect,

in their hands, and choked up,
because it was any feet
poking out of the bedclothes.

And when the calm, pinched,
twenty-year-old face
came free, and he lay there,

five foot four of authentic
Victorian adventurer, tuberculous,
malnourished: John Torrington

the stoker, who came so far
in the cold, and someone whispered,
It's like he's unconscious.

Then Beattie stooped, lifted him
out of bed, the six stone
limp in his arms, and the head lolled

and rested on his shoulder,
and he felt the rush
that reckless trust sends

through parents and lovers. To have him
like that, the frail, diseased
little time-traveller,

to feel the lashes prickle
your cheek, to be that close
to the parted lips:

you would know all the fairy-tales
spoke true; how could you not try
to wake him with a kiss?

Graffiti Man

Flint scratched a stick-man
into stone: me. A wavy spear
perched on its hand: *me hunting.*

He torched his way across continents,
Als'kander, Iskandar, Sikandar
founding Alexandrias.

He wrote his name on diseases,
roses and children, scribbled it in neon
across skyscrapers,

spiked programs with its virus.
He sprayed it on ohms, sandwiches,
wellingtons, dahlias, hoovers.

White columns, grey stones, black walls,
heavy with names beyond number.
Such a one died

in war, of AIDS, from old age.
I, Kallaischros, lie
in the restless sea,

no-one knows where, and this stone
lies too, marking the place
where I am not.

Leningrad's gone, and Rhodesia,
scrubbed off the stone.
Ideas are harder

to clean; names won't come loose
from a phrase of music,
a story, a law, a faith,

but you need a keen edge
to carve them. Most settle
for a can of spray-paint.

On every stretch of sand
stick-swirled patterns
waiting for the tide,

on every snowfield
the definition of footprints
crumbling in the sun,

on every window
words, fading on the brief
page of mist.

Segunders are named each day,
and if you breathe on the window,
the words come back.

Ikon

In her mind an ikon
glows, a dark-eyed face.
It was painted straight on
to the wall; if she cuts it out
now, she must take plaster
and all, and leave its shape
in the bare brick.

Postcard

Seal in the voe, dark head, I thought of you;
skuas diving on fulmars, I don't trust
your lover. Thrift clings in the rock clefts,
and I worry about your debts.

Water so clear, I can see gannets fishing;
air too ruthlessly pure to screen out the sun.
Innocence burns. I touch your face in my pocket
and ache with the brightness.

Saw the aurora last night; the shivering wave
of lights, of not-quite-colours too subtle to name,
drifting over the dark, like a transient smile
kindling grave eyes.

Rather

Anything rather than say
                your eyes deceived you,
that the high peak
             was never out of reach,
or that a man was less
              than your thoughts made him.
Say it the once,
        and you would always see it
that way;
        you would look out over waste acres,
never once shaping
           in rank weeds and litter
the swell of trees,
        a fountain's glittering arc,
sunflowers turning slowly,
           the scent of apples.

Far Places

So he made it, in the end, to the top
of the west ridge, half an hour longer
by the road, while his sons went straight up
and waited for him, lounging on the heather,

laughing. He saw the mica in the rock
once more, flashing silver in the sun,
and thought, as he paused to get his breath back,
I couldn't stand not seeing it again.

And then the haul, over miles of hill
and moorland, stumbling in and out
of peat cuttings, watching his footing, while
they strode so far ahead, he couldn't shout

to them. Out of sight. He knew he'd find them
where he had led them all those years ago,
by the steep waterfall. They'd wait for him,
watching the water mist and cream and rainbow,

as mesmerised as ever. He'd rest a minute,
then scramble down beside them in the spray,
or maybe not; the view from the green height
was good enough for most folks. Either way,

it would be worth the walk, the tiredness,
to look again and feel it stop his heart.
But every distant, high, uncommon place
is getting further, harder, more effort

for the same prize. *One day*, the thought nags,
you'll say no. Not got the lungs: too stiff.
Or it won't be the breath, the back, the legs,
but the will. And his throat clamps with grief

for the far places, snapshots in a frame,
dim memories, a shard of silver rock
turned in the hand. The glint isn't the same
out of the sun; you never get it back.

The Garden

Outside the window is a field,
and in that field sheep graze,
backs to the wind, fleece blown forward
off their bare buttocks. Brent geese
pick around them, quicker, bright-eyed,
wide boys among the yokels. And rabbits
crop, sniff the air, drop back down,
stiffen again, living on the edge
of panic, while dapper oystercatchers
in black and white dodge between
webbed feet and cloven.

                  Open the window,
the rabbits will be a flash of white scut;
step out of doors, the oystercatchers
will take flight. As you walk toward them,
sheep back their lambs away. The geese
may front up, a hissing phalanx. They'll shuffle off
in the end. It takes no time
to empty a field.

The Tormented Censor

He sees what is not given to others:
the foreign magazines, before they are made
fit for the faithful. He makes them fit.

All day long, he sifts indecent women.
Runner's World, his glinting scissors meet
and part, amputate bare legs and arms.

All through *Hello!* his soft felt-tip is busy
stroking a chador of thick black ink
over celebrity cleavages.

Even in *Woman's Weekly* some minx
moistens her lips with the tip of a pink tongue;
he rips it out. The whole page.

They all get shredded, the silky limbs,
the taut breasts, flesh cut to ribbons.
He is devout, and keeps none back.

But after work, walking home, if a woman
should pass, decently veiled, all in black,
his muscles tense; he tries not to look

as the little devils in his mind whisper
what they know, melt cloth, draw curves
on her dark shapelessness.

The City of Empty Rooms

There's a city above the city, above street level,
above the blankets wheezing in doorways,
above the window-dressers' tableaux
and the "sale" signs, above the gold lettering
of the third-floor solicitors, higher yet,

the city of empty rooms. They're carpeted
in deep-pile dust, wall-to-wall silence,
cavity isolation. *Secluded residence*
commanding extensive views. No parking.
Pollsters and canvassers don't climb this far,

no census-takers nor rent collectors.
The city in the air was never surveyed,
the *Rough Guide* missed it out; no-one has studied
its population, its mythology.
Up there, anything might be possible,

maybe the hidden roof-slopes are covered
in gardens; maybe the empty rooms are there
for those who need them, and the gentle murmur
from all the eaves: *loving, loving, loving*
is the voice not of pigeons but of doves.

Pause: Rewind

Nowadays the dead walk and talk
in the wedding video, the camcorded break,

the fuzzed black-and-white of security cameras.
A policeman watches as two balaclavas

burst, again and again, through the door
of an off-licence, and the old shopkeeper

panics, blunders into a baseball bat,
slumps in his blood. Before things can get

any worse, the young PC presses 'pause',
then 'rewind'. And the dark stream flows

into the head again; the old fellow
gets up. The thieves are backing jerkily through

the door, which closes on them. All right,
all tidy. This could get to be a habit:

so many tapes he could whizz backwards.
That bus and bike, speeding to the crossroads,

will not collide, the drunk at the hotel
will stop short of his car, the young girl

will never disappear down the subway
where her rapist waits so patiently.

Pause: rewind. Freeze-frame where you want
the world to stop. The moment before the moment,

before Challenger leaves the launch pad,
before the boat sails or the letter's posted,

before the singer jumps off the bridge,
before you see the face that ends your marriage,

before the pink suit is dyed red,
before a thought is formed or a word said.

Bolshies

In the last days of a lost war,
a man occupying a Brussels office
made time for spite, signed an order
to send one final trainload down the line
to the death camps. And his secretary
typed it, and a clerk bespoke the train,
and policemen who had no heart for the job
loaded the prisoners anyway.

But then it was all down to the lads
on the line: the drivers, the signalmen,
the track gangs, and all of a sudden
pointas seized up, urgent repairs took days,
you couldn't lay your hands on spare parts.
Wrong-set signals sent the train trundling
in circles, while the bolshie branch rep
wheeled out his trusty, well-oiled excuses.

And when peace finally turned up
ahead of the spare parts, when the prisoners
could all change trains, and the bosses commenced
awarding themselves medals, the lads went back
to looking out for each other, fiddling timesheets,
arguing over demarcation lines,
doing their best to baulk each jack-in-office
who tried to make the trains run on time.

Unkindness

A dead man is so like to a man sleeping,
whispered the professor, when she laid eyes
on the gentle face a peat-spade turned over
in Tollund bog. The centuries-old unkindness

that buried him there had only marked his brow
with little furrows, like a man's in a dream.
He lay relaxed on his side. She almost thought
she could have shaken his shoulder and woken him.

So I feel, seeing you lie, somewhat stiffer
than usual, so that lifting your slight weight
is no such easy matter. I can't notice
anything missing, no, not even the light

of wit in your open eyes. There is just the stiffness,
and a little crust of dried blood at the mouth,
and is that any reason to leave a kind companion
alone for an iron age in the black earth?

Crossing the Bridge

He was on his way
to buy a wedding ring,
singing as he went.

Crossing Cardiff Bridge,
he met his old love,
and they fell in talk,

she wished him joy
of his wedding, and said
it was fine weather

for the time of year,
and his whole heart
went out to her.

Between water and air,
country and town,
the world alters:

not here but there,
not Elizabeth but Joan,
not what I thought,

but what surprised me.
He stood on a bridge
and let it happen,

or made it happen;
who knows how
these bridges work,

though we stand so often
on a stone moment,
an arc of choice

or chance. Sometimes
we are Joan, the mover,
the change in the air,

sometimes the left-behind,
so much Elizabeth
under the bridge,

sometimes the man
in the middle, transfixed
by a shining word,

sun on his face,
the sweet certainty
that crossing the bridge

will change everything
for better or worse,
and he can't go back.

Note: From an incident in William Thomas's *Diaries, 1762-1795*, pub. The Cardiff South Wales Record Society 1995. Harry Edward went to buy the ring for his wedding to Elizabeth Water. Crossing the bridge into Cardiff, he met his old love Joan Morgan, and before he was over the bridge had decided to marry her instead, which he did.

From *The Beautiful Lie*

The Beautiful Lie

He was about four, I think... it was so long ago.
In a garden: he'd done some damage
behind a bright screen of sweet-peas
– snapped a stalk, a stake, I don't recall,
but the grandmother came and saw, and asked him:
"Did you do that?"

Now, if she'd said *why* did you do that,
he'd never have denied it. She showed him
he had a choice. I could see in his face
the new sense, the possible. That word and deed
need not match, that you could say the world
different, to suit you.

When he said "No", I swear it was as moving
as the first time a baby's fist clenches
on a finger, as momentous as the first
taste of fruit. I could feel his eyes looking
through a new window, at a world whose form
and colour weren't fixed

but fluid, that poured like a snake, trembled
around the edges like northern lights, shape-shifted
at the spell of a voice. I could sense him filling
like a glass, hear the unreal sea in his ears.
This is how to make songs, create men, paint pictures,
tell a story.

I think I made up the screen of sweet peas.
Maybe they were beans, maybe there was no screen:
it just felt as if there should be, somehow.
And he was my – no, I don't need to tell that.
I know I made up the screen. And I recall very well
what he had done.

The Lit Room

i.m. George Mackay Brown

There was a flat
on a long street by the sea,
a room, scarcely lit,

a head of clay,
sunken-eyed, cheekbones hollowed,
a memento mori

for the face that glowed
from the shadows: so gaunt, so mobile.
There was a word

someone let fall,
that filled him, all of a sudden,
with light. A vessel

of ware so thin,
the wine shone through. Light leaks
into the ocean

when the clay cracks,
into the dark. Who notices
if the street lacks

one lamp, one face?
These days, the room is empty
of shadows,

well-lit, tidy.
There is a flat, on a long street
by the sea....

Fanfic

Fanfic is a sequence of poems about the interface between fiction and reality, and how fictional characters acquire a degree of reality via their fans' belief in them. It is set in the world of fan fiction and the notes at the end are for those to whom the vocabulary of that world is unfamiliar.

Fanfic

This game is old. Listen
to a story – Robin Hood, maybe,
all in the greenwood.

Toy figures become outlaws.
Nottingham Castle grows
from Lego, turns into Camelot,

a Batcave, a flight deck,
and the words are made flesh
over and over.

But stories end
and most children
put their toys away.

This game comes next. Some
never learn it. Run out
of stories, make more stories.

Take the plastic men
and paint their features
with grief, plans, memories.

Whatever you can think,
they can do. The storyteller
can close his spell-book.

You're time-served now; you know
the magic words.
You have the con.

Alternate

Well, she was tired, I suppose;
she'd been up watching videos till late

and she wasn't really interested,
but I nuzzled, made a pest

of myself, and she played along,
sleepily. No spark, but I needed

the closeness. I'll take what's on offer,
these days. Then she goes all soft

suddenly, relaxes, kisses back,
and I miss a breath. But she's looking

past me somehow, and I know
the look: I know what she's doing.

She's making a what if, rewriting
the script. This man, not that....

and she moves like water, and it's perfect,
except it's all for him. I hold her,

not speaking, because it's not my voice
that belongs with this. I'd only

spoil it for her. I let him come
in my body, pulsing, foaming,

eyes full of stars. Then I turn and lie
facing away, because I'm crying.

Missing Scenes

She knows at once the spaces
where stories grow. The chance mention
of some frontier planet,

or a lost love. Something unresolved.
Five days a man spends off-camera.
Whatever happens

out of sight, implied in a glance,
she can fill the gap. She sees them
everywhere now,

the missing scenes; she can't read
a book or watch a film
 without shaping sequels,

nor leave a man or woman
a corner of shadow
or a blank page.

That day off sick, the week
away on business, who knows?
What couldn't you do

in three years at college, twenty
in a crap job, a fortnight's
escape each summer?

When she thinks, these days,
of her life, it seems to be
all missing scenes

where something should have happened,
but when she looks for the stories,
they won't come.

Cross-Reality

If she can Mary-Sue into his world,
can he to hers? She likes to fancy

how it would happen. The co-ordinates
screw up, land him in Tesco Metro

by the clingfilm.... would he be wearing
that sprayed-on leather suit? Somehow

she's the only one who knows him,
lost in her world, trying not to look it.

She takes his hand, finds him a quiet spot
in the car park, gets a dark-eyed smile

as his outline dissolves into light.
She goes home with his imprint on her eyes.

There'd need to be some fissure, she supposes,
in the fabric of time, some spark

jumping the tracks from one universe
to its parallel.... would lightning do it?

But her favourite theory is simply
that if she believes in him enough,

belief will call him like a gravitational pull
across realities, harden his edges

– made of words and light as he is –
into flesh she can touch without a doubt.

If electronic signals add up to a picture
on a screen, then why not stories, images

from many minds to a man? What is belief
but the need for something to be true?

If she waits long enough, he will stand before her,
and she will tell him: *Our waiting brought you.*

Lost

She is searching all the worlds:
Lycos, GoTo, AltaVista,

for his planetfalls, sites
with traces of him.

She lights, sparrowlike, on crumbs
of fact: a grainy picture, a quote,

now and then his voice on tape,
the icy purr that undoes her.

She gives herself time to taste
the shiver, then jerks her thumb

to jump to the next link.
She trawls a virtual bookshelf

for transcripts: each episode
of his life is out there, if you know

where to look, and she knows.
There is always one link further,

another angle, someone else writing
a novel treatment, a sequel

to the final series.... The web
won't let him die, but where is he?

A suit, a screenplay, an actor's voice,
a memory, a spin-off in the minds

that won't let go, that want him
young and travelling for ever.

Sometimes she senses no limit
to him, no end to his story.

The actor, earthbound, has long worn
new suits, new skins. She avoids

all sight of him. It's not him,
the lost young man, any more

than the shape she lives in now
is the one she knows

from old photographs. It's all
out there somewhere. Armed

with her Favourites file, she shortcuts
cyberforests, questions the masters

of knowledge, forgets to eat.
She is tired: her eyes hurt: she scrolls on.

Notes to *Fanfic*

Alternate: Fanfic (q.v.) story which postulates an alternative to something that happened in the source. E.g. Cathy marries Heathcliff.

Cross-reality: (also crossover; cross-universe). Genre of fanfic (q.v.) which mixes characters from different fictions, (Princess Leia meets Dracula), or fictional characters and real life.

Fanfic: a.k.a. fan fiction. Stories about fictional characters from TV, film, novels etc, written by the fans of those characters, for love rather than profit; found in fanzines and on the Net.

Mary-Sue: Fanfic story where the female lead is not a character from the series/film/whatever, but represents the author.

Missing Scene: Fanfic story which fills in a gap in the original where information was withheld or not spelled out.

Making Contact

Some sailor-artist sketched it as it happened:
two ships anchored off a new shore,
the Inuit waiting, intrigued, up the beach,
Parry and Ross, backed by a small party
discreetly armed, stepping forward in friendship
to offer the chief (or the foremost idler,
for all they know) their age-old token
of peace the world over: an olive branch.

Parry is holding it out, his metaphor,
and getting nowhere; nobody seems to want
the other end. But Ross is looking round,
taking in a landscape bare of green
to the paper's edge, knowing not a bush
nor tree has ever grown there, and you can see
he's going to turn, any moment, to Parry:
Edward, we might need to rethink this one.

And then they'll give presents, arrive
at an understanding. Parry will write, later,
of thieving primitives with depraved morals.
He himself will be handed down in story
as the idiot who couldn't build a snow house,
didn't know that food was for sharing,
nor how to accept graciously the loan
of a wife.

But for now, for this moment
while he prods the chill air with his olive
and stares into polite blank eyes,
while gestures fall flat and words translate
into gibberish, his helpless shrug mirrors
the other's rueful grin. Reaching out,
missing, balked, wordless, they will never be
so close again.

Going to Liverpool

I am a middle-aged woman
travelling on business
and I'm going to Liverpool,

where I'll take time out
to visit Albert Dock
and the museum

where my youth is preserved.
The fashions I followed,
the songs I knew by heart,

the faces that convulsed
my own into screams
and sobs, they'll all be there.

I'm going to Liverpool,
and it is autumn.
The fields outside Leominster

lie in stubble, the leaves
of Ludlow's trees are jaundiced
and flushed with the fever

that says they're finished.
The ticket collector
said *Thank you, Madam.*

My daughter's grown up
and my mother's dead,
and between the pages

of the notebook
where I'm writing this
I keep a yellowed ticket

to a match, a picture
of an actor, Edwin Morgan's reply
to my fan letter,

and I'm going to Liverpool
because I'm the kind
that always will.

The Boy with a Cloud in his Hand

He hasn't got much: not a roof,
nor a job, nor any great hopes,
but he's got a cloud in his hand
and he thinks he might squeeze
till the rain falls over the town,
and he thinks he might tease
the cottonwool fluff into strands
of thin mist, and blank everything out,
and he thinks he might blow
this dandelion clock so high,
it will never come down, and he thinks
he might eat it, a taste of marshmallow
sliding inside him, filling him up
with emptiness, till he's all space,
and he thinks, when he's hollow and full,
he might float away.

Lady Franklin's Man

I never can be a happy person, because I live too much in others
— Lady Jane Franklin

In 1845 Sir John Franklin, aged 59, led an expedition to the Arctic to complete the North-West Passage. When, after two years, he had not returned, the Admiralty began a massive search. By the early 1850s, with little found, they were ready to abandon it. Lady Franklin, conscious that men from earlier expeditions had survived years in the Arctic, opposed this. She financed ships herself and persuaded others to, but to do this, and to keep the Admiralty searching, she needed public opinion on her side, which she gained by cultivating Franklin's image as an Arctic hero.

Lady Franklin Recalls a Flag
1845

A few days before you sailed,
we were sitting up
after dark. We fell quiet; I think
you were almost asleep,

and I was stitching your flag
by the light from the fire.
You'd had a chill. I looked up
and saw you shiver,

and a tenderness shook me all through.
I knelt on the mat
and draped the flag over your knees
to keep the cold out.

And you started, wide-eyed: "Don't you know
only a dead man
has *that* thrown over him?"
You looked so drawn,

so shaky, your face of a sudden
grey, and I thought: *how long
since those lines came? How many years
has he not been young?*

Lady Franklin Begins To Be Concerned
1847

When first you sailed, all my pictures of you
were bright. I could fancy all your lines
smoothing away in the wind, the northern light
you love so well.

That stiffness in your shoulder would start to ease
with action; even the headaches would fade
as the hate-filled faces of Hobart
fell back in your wake.

And you would go forward, west until west
became east, until nameless channels
became safe passage, until a private man,
a man who shunned fame,

a man who'd blow a fly off his hand
rather than kill it, became a hero.
The man I love. I have always known
it was there in you,

under the gentleness. People forget,
seeing you at a desk or in an armchair,
what an adventurer you were. The man
who ate his boots,

who starved and lived… I was glad of your sailing,
that May morning, a white dove at your mast,
knowing you'd come back whole, healed, yourself
as you were meant to be.

But now the third winter is drawing down,
and no sign. Are you iced-in
up there, like Ross, watching the sun set,
knowing it won't rise

for months? Those men came back with a taste
for seal-fat, speaking little, afraid of the dark,
sharing no memories. Who will you be
when you come home?

Lady Franklin at Muckle Flugga
1849

I suppose you must have passed this place
as you sailed north: the last lighthouse
in the kingdom. I can hear you saying
– if this letter reaches you at all –
"Whatever is she doing up there?"
Well, I came to the northern isles
to meet the whalers on their way home
from Greenland. I thought I might find one
who'd seen you, had news of you.

I know now that they haven't. They are kind,
so kind, but they can tell me nothing.
I could have gone home weeks ago,
but I stayed in Lerwick, sending letters
by every northbound captain – I wonder
if you ever saw one?

                Up here, they have
a different sky – well, you knew that,
but I did not. I could hardly believe it
after London: this high, vast vault
with three levels of cloud, and the air
pure enough to drink… I knew
it must be this sky you were seeing,
and it felt so clear, as if I could call
to you and be heard over any distance,
as if I could reach into the deep blue
and touch you.

              That was why
I came here, I think, farther north still,
to the last lighthouse. I wanted to be
a few miles closer, as if it could help.
Mr Edmondston understood; he is a good man.
He showed me the little rock, the Out Stack,
beyond here, even, the northernmost point
on our soil. I looked so long, and he knew
my mind, and rowed me there.

                              So I stood
where I think few ever went, or wanted to,
southwards a whole country at my back
and northwards – what? Ocean, sky, nothing
to break or change them. The nothing,
the emptiness, you sailed into.

It is night now, but not dark:
these are the blue summer nights
you told me of, and I am writing this
by a window at the Edmondstons'
without lamp or candle. It will sail
with some captain, perhaps to find you,
perhaps not. But today on that rock
I was so close to you, I knew
we could not be closer in a bed.

Lady Franklin Refuses To Wear Mourning
1851

Eleanor, please don't think ill of me.
Do you suppose I like wearing pink

at my age? I never liked it much
– a sickly colour. And as for this bright green…

But it shouts to all and sundry: *I believe*
he is alive. Unless I show that,

they'll give him up for lost. I need them
to pester *The Times*, sign petitions,

write cheques, make speeches. Men have lived
years out there. They *must* go on searching,

and they will, if I keep them in mind
of him. The legend, the traveller

in hard places, the hero in the ice:
he has to live for them. The right words,

acts, gestures, dress, could bring him back,
as sure as magic, but if I make

one mistake, the spell will not work:
you know how it is in stories.

It must be the right lamp, the right lips
kissing the sleeper, the right words exactly,

or the door stays closed. The door
to men's hearts, to the Admiralty's purse,

to the ice, to him. Who will conjure it open
if not me, in my mountebank's cloak?

Lady Franklin and the Kindness of Strangers
1853

Little adventurer, I am sorry.
I have been all night crying for you,

my poor René. That the ice should take
one so warm-hearted. You were too young,

I should never have let you risk your life,
and twice, at that. You were hardly home

before you shipped again, for a man
you had never seen. What kindness I find

in men. Mr Kennedy leaves his business
to look after itself in Canada.

Dr Kane, who knows he will not live
to see forty, takes his weak heart north,

when he might rest in comfort. Even Ross –
impossible man, but when I think

how he sailed, so old, on such a journey....
And you, my dear, come from your home in France

in such haste; who loved dancing and laughter,
to die in a cold sea. Edward told me

the crew wept for you; he could barely speak
himself. I told him he, at least,

must not go north a third time: I would see
no more young lives lost. He just looked

from under those dark brows of his:
"I would go out again. He would have, too."

I wonder if so many men have gone
questing like this since Arthur reigned a king,

if he ever did. A kind man draws
kindness from others: a brave man

helps them find courage. Up there, they say,
under the ice, in the dark of the dead winter,

lies the magnetic pole that attracts all
the shivering needles northward.

Lady Franklin Hears a Ballad in the Street
1857

I heard that song again today.
The coalman whistling on his cart
left his breath on the frosty air
and the notes sparkled down our street

to a young girl scrubbing her step.
Ten thousand pounds I would gladly give,
she crooned... A shop-lad took it up:
... to know on earth Lord Franklin lives.

And, as ever, the word jars.
He is no lord, I want to call:
just plain Sir John.... I bite it back.
I am too glad to hear your tale

still on their lips, your name spoken,
to quarrel with a misplaced word.
I can guess why they call you so:
where there's a Lady, there's a Lord,

so they must think. It is my fault:
knowing my name, they change yours,
and I am known. I am the one
who makes the speeches, writes the letters:

you are unseen behind the ice,
oceans and years away, a man
of story, an adventurer's quest.
Some child will ask me, now and then,

if you are real or "just in books".
Your name has floated free of you,
a phrase of song upon the air.
All down the street, I hear your echo.

Lady Franklin Receives News
1859

I did not think you could have left the world,
and I not know it. I thought I would feel your death
like a lack of warmth or food: I am cold, I am hungry,
I am a widow. I thought it would be like that.

June the eleventh, eighteen-forty-seven…
I had to look back in my diaries
to know what kind of a day that was,
the day a gap closed up where you had stood,

and I find it was like any Friday.
I left my card, answered a few letters,
wondered if you were on your way back.
I hadn't even started to worry.

And you were dying – of what? I wish the note
had said. An accident, an illness?
At least, then, most of your officers
were still alive. I hope they were with you.

I hope someone, Crozier or Fitzjames,
held you in his arms. I hope someone
spoke to you, told you *I'm here*, all through.
I hope you never felt alone.

All the time I was raising money,
fitting out ships, begging the Admiralty
to send more men in search, you were not there.
When I stood on the rock and felt you close,

on the empty ocean, you were not there.
When poor René Bellot gave his life,
when street-lads sang your ballad, when *The Times*
said every boy in Britain knew your name,

you were nowhere. Or in the boys' mouths,
in the ballad, in the minds of men
like René, Edward, William Kennedy,
Captain M'Clintock.... I should like to think

they went because you were somewhere,
not nowhere, that you drew them north.
René told me he knew no class or nation
up there, that all men were his brothers.

Perhaps you – *that* you – are still somewhere;
the you who made that happen. The man
who'll have a statue, a plaque in the Abbey,
a place in story. That man won't die,

but I am thinking now of the man
who hated to see anyone hurt,
whose toes were always cold, who liked his tea
so much. That man will be in no ballads:

I am not sure anyone would believe
in him now, but I knew him, and he died
on June the eleventh, eighteen-forty-seven,
and whoever was near him, I was not.

Lady Franklin Resumes Her Travels

1860-69

New York
Loud voices, brash ways,
with kind hearts. You would like them,
if you could know them.

Brazil
Cruel. Bright. Poor folk
at the rich men's carnival.
Hobart with music.

Patagonia
Wind blowing over
an empty land: who would choose
that sound to die to?

California
They are still digging
for gold here: may all men find
what they most search for.

British Columbia
Canoes took us up
the Fraser, Indian-paddled,
like you, long ago.

Hawaii
Girls, mission-dressed, eyes
cast down, hands and feet tracing
forbidden dances.

Japan
The locked land opened
to your name: I was honoured
to carry it there.

Singapore
Straight streets, prim manners.
Who travelled so far, to make
the place they came from?

Suez
Cranes and great dredgers
sucking sea, shaping land; what
can hinder men now?

Dalmatia

Harsh coast, fishermen
who feed all strangers. I hope
you met men like these.

Germany

The view took my breath,
but I went up by litter.
Age: the worst mountain.

France

The Exhibition:
the world's eyes on this city.
René should be here.

India

Ten feet up, swaying,
feeling sick, on this grey deck,
this elephant-ship.

N.W. Africa

Dark archways lengthen,
tempt. The best road is risky,
the best place unknown.

Lady Franklin Fails To Write an Epitaph
1875

Words fail me, they say… When I needed
to persuade, I could make words serve me:

that is why your monument is building
in the Abbey. Your name where it belongs,

in stone, in glory. It is what I wanted
for you. Yet now, given the chance

to write words for it, I cannot.
Four lines to say what you were:

I have written twelve-page letters
telling the world that, and now

I can shape nothing. You'd laugh:
you were the shy, the tongue-tied one.

The Laureate is writing it – I think
he calls you "heroic sailor-soul",

but to me he is always the lad
who annoyed you, all those years ago,

by putting his feet on the furniture –
not that you said. You left words to me,

but words have left me, now. I feel tired,
these days. I walk with a staff,

like some old wizard, but I make
no magic. Perhaps my spirits are gone

at last. The words must be right,
exactly right, or things will not happen….

Notes to Lady Franklin's Man

Lady Franklin Begins To Be Concerned
"Hobart" Not long before, Franklin had been a most unhappy governor of
Tasmania. He and Lady Franklin had, by trying to improve the lot of the
convict and aborigine inhabitants, attracted the hostile contempt of the
British expatriates who made up Hobart society. The appointment ended
early: Franklin returned to England close to nervous exhaustion and, so he
thought, with his reputation damaged. That was why he agreed to go
north.

"Ross" Sir John Ross, some years earlier, had been trapped four years in
Arctic ice but brought home 19 of his 22 men alive and fairly well.

Lady Franklin at Muckle Flugga
"Mr Edmondston" Keeper, at the time, of the Muckle Flugga light off
Shetland.

Lady Franklin Refuses to Wear Mourning
"Eleanor" Franklin's daughter by his first wife.

Lady Franklin and the Kindness of Strangers
"René" Lt Joseph-René Bellot of the French navy, who had obtained leave
to go searching for Franklin at his own expense. He was 27, endearingly
affectionate, and Lady Franklin treated him as a son.

"so old" The Admiralty refused to send Sir John Ross to search for
Franklin, on the grounds that he was 73. He went anyway, financing his
own ship and running up debts of £500, because he'd given Franklin his
word that he would.

"Edward" Commander Edward Inglefield, on loan from the Navy to one
of Lady Franklin's expeditions. He, like Bellot, had been out twice for her
and refused her offers of pay.

Lady Franklin Receives News
In 1859 Captain Leopold M'Clintock returned from yet another search
financed by Lady Franklin, (the Admiralty had bowed out by then), with
evidence of the expedition's fate, including a note found in a cairn which
confirmed that Franklin had died in 1847.

Lady Franklin Resumes Her Travels
Lady Franklin was a great traveller all her life; this itinerary from one decade is, believe it or not, selective.

Lady Franklin Fails to Write an Epitaph
"The Laureate" Tennyson, Franklin's nephew by marriage, came up with this:

Not here! the white north has thy bones; and thou,
Heroic sailor-soul,
Art passing on thine happier voyage now
Toward no earthly pole.

One can only wish Lady Franklin had trusted herself to do the job. She died, aged 83, before the monument was completed, which gave the Dean of Westminster the chance to add a few lines commemorating her. His prose put Tennyson's verse to shame:

"...this monument was erected by Jane, his widow, who, after long waiting, and sending many in search of him, herself departed to seek and to find him in the realms of light."

Survivor

Forty-five years ago
you didn't die: you were famous
for staying alive.

You were sixteen.
On Pathé; black hair rumpled
against a white stretcher,

you looked like Elvis.
Whatever you'd done; whatever
the witless bravado,

the violence, your eyes
gazed wide and dark. Bone structure
to die for.

You were beautiful
the way a young man is sometimes
for a few years,

no more. That transience
glows through the skin, says *Now,*
take it now,

there's no tomorrow.
Nor there was, I know, for the man
you killed, nor the man

who died for you –
I'm not forgetting. But when
I see the shots

of you now: the paunch,
the grey hair thinning, the skin
dulled and slackened

with sixty-one years,
it seems there is death, and death,
and against my will

my mind does not run
on the brave nor the innocent.
I am mourning

your moment long gone,
your worthless, ephemeral face
that coarsened quickly

in some prison,
that would have coarsened slowly
in any case.

Lockerbie Butter

Scottish hotels serve it in small wrapped portions,
to go with plastic thimblefuls of jam
or marmalade, and no-one bats an eyelid.
I did see someone, once, notice the name

and blench, and I thought he might ask
"Say, is that the place where the plane fell
out of the sky?" But he didn't; he spread it
on his toast, went on as usual,

as people do. A plane, miles above,
is blown apart, gouges a burning crater
where, just lately, folk were going about
their lives, seeing to some daily matter,

when all their days were torn in one handful
out of the calendar. And what was once
a name on a station, a map, a packet,
comes to mean murder, grief, cosmic mischance.

At first its people stumble through the wreck
of logic, dazed, asking *why us?*
By and by, being marked out for sorrow
turns to comfort. They put on grace, conscious

of cameras, strangers, the eyes of the dead:
they live on levels where they had not known
they could breathe. Soon the press-pack will tire
of heroes, write *Feud In Tragedy Town,*

then move out, leaving them to go back
to normal. Yet even in the first days,
while the great scar still throbbed, while fields bore
children's belongings, while widows hugged space,

some folk were out milking incurious cows,
which pause no more for grief than does the sun.
Milk comes twice a day and spoils quickly
if not attended to; things go on,

and someone told me once how he froze,
(on holiday, just wandering around),
to see musicians play some pretty waltz
under their banner: Dachau Town Band.

Well, they could change the name... but if a name
could make it not the place of death, why then
it wouldn't be the place of birth either,
their birth, I mean, nor that of any man

who ever led a decent life there,
whose word was good, who was a careful father
or a kind son, who spoke against wrong,
who made others long to live better.

A meadow pastures cattle: soldiers come
and soak it red, lime it with their youth,
and by and by, as dust and distance take them,
the flattened grass rises in their path,

and it grows from bones and grief and courage
and agony: the dead are in each blade,
and they are not diminished nor forgotten
in its unfailing greenness: all they did

and felt and suffered is in memory,
in the neighbourhood, the ground, the town,
in daffodils blazing round the Clifford Tower,
in the children of Dunblane, Aberfan,

in every note of music played in Dachau
and in these oblongs: death turned to grass,
grass turned to milk, milk turned to a living,
the small gold ingots of the commonplace.

Night Nurses in the Morning

No bench in the bus shelter; they slump
against caving perspex, dragging the Silk Cut

deep into their lungs, eyes closed, holding
the moment, then letting a long breath go.

And they don't talk. Swollen ankles above
big white boat-shoes, dreams of foot-spas.

Pale pink pale green pale blue, even without
the washed-out uniforms you could tell them

from us other early-morning faces
going in, starting the day. We eye them sideways

as they fall into seats, ease their shoes off.
More pallid than colliers or snooker players,

the vampires of mercy. All their haunts lie near
this bus route: here's St Stephen's Hospice,

where folk go to die; there, the Lennox Home
for Elderly Ladies. Just round the bend,

the other granny-park, where I walked past
an open window one evening when the lilac

was out, and heard a young voice scream, over and over,
You bitch, you bitch, and another tone,

querulous and high, a complaining descant
to her theme. They both sounded desperate.

People who live by night aren't quite canny.
We let them keep things running, avoid their eyes,

resenting the way they don't seem to need us there.
What do you do, in the corners of darkness

where we sweep the inconvenient? What is it
you never say to each other on the bus?

As our faces wake, exhaustion silvers
the backs of their eyes: not windows but mirrors.

The Pursuit of Happiness

.... certain unalienable rights... among these
are life, liberty and the pursuit of happiness...
– Thomas Jefferson:
The American Declaration of Independence, 1776

But he only said
you had a right to chase it:
he never mentioned

catching it up.
Like that coyote,
forever in pursuit

of the road-runner,
forever unpacking
the latest gadget

from Acme, sure
it'll work, this time,
you walk, unerring,

off cliff edges,
into tunnels that echo
with oncoming trains.

The gun backfires; the fuse
is a simmering dud,
till you pick it up.

All feet but yours
escape the traps.
You wait, exactly

where the rock will fall,
watching, far off,
the dust of your dreams:

then it's back
to the Sears & Roebuck
for another miracle.

And if you caught it,
if you ever did,
wouldn't it taste stringy,

all muscle and disappointment,
and what would you do
with the rest of your life?

Easter

Outside the library
the old drinkers rock
and hug themselves,

crying softly, cursing,
and the snow falls
in slow motion

through the bloom
of a flowering cherry.
April showers.

A man stumbles
on his wavy line
across ground that glitters,

his tread crunching
snow crystals, broken glass
and white petals

that bruise to a faint
pink smear behind him,
as if he walked barefoot.

The Extra

I forget which film
(black-and-white, thirties)
has a crowd scene,

a liner leaving port,
and among the extras
at the ship's rail

stands an old man
with a rather distinctive hat
and a wistful face,

waving his farewells
to the extras on shore,
among whom,

with a rather distinctive hat,
by some continuity cock-up
he also stands.

I hope the director
didn't give him hell
for wrecking the shot,

because no moment
has moved me more.
So many voyagers

since the world began,
leaving one self, one country,
one life, for another,

and never a man
embarks, without looking back
at what stays behind:

the face, translucent
as a sloughed snakeskin,
the thin figure,

fading at the edges,
who raises a hand
slowly, in a gesture

that aches in the bones
all the way
to the other side.

Toast

When I'm old, I'll say *the summer*
they built the stadium. And I won't mean

the council. I'll be hugging the memory
of how, open to sun and the judgement

of passing eyes, young builders lay
golden and melting on hot pavements,

the toast of Cardiff. Each blessed lunchtime
Westgate Street, St John's, the Hayes

were lined with fit bodies; forget
the jokes, these jeans were fuzz stretched tight

over unripe peaches. Sex objects,
and happily up for it. When women

sauntered by, whistling, they'd bask
in warm smiles, browning slowly, loving

the light. Sometimes they'd clock men
looking them over. It made no odds,

they never got mad; it was too heady
being young and fancied and in the sun.

They're gone now, all we have left of them
this vast concrete-and-glass mother-ship

that seems to have landed awkwardly
in our midst. And Westgate's dark

with November rain, but different, as if
the stones retain heat, secret impressions

of shoulder-blades, shallow cups,
as sand would do. The grey façade

of the empty auction house, three storeys
of boarded windows, doesn't look sad,

more like it's closed its eyes, breathing in
the smell of sweat, sunblock, confidence.

From *The Movement of Bodies*

Times Like Places

There are times like places: there is weather
the shape of moments. Dark afternoons
by a fire are Craster in the rain
and a pub they happened on, unlooked-for
and welcoming, while a North Sea gale
spat spume at the rattling windows.

And most August middays can take him
to the village in Sachsen-Anhalt,
its windows shuttered against the sun,
and a hen sleeping in the dusty road,
the day they picked cherries in a garden
so quiet, they could hear each other breathe.

Nor can he ever be on a ferry,
looking back at a boat's wake, and not think
of the still, glassy morning off the Hook,
when it dawned on him they didn't talk
in sentences any more: didn't need to,
each knowing what the other would say.

The worst was Aberdeen, when they walked
the length of Union Street not speaking,
choking up, glancing sideways at each other,
but never at the same time. Black cats
and windy bridges bring it all back,
eyes stinging. Yet even this memory

is dear to him, now that no place or weather
or time of day can happen to them both.
On clear winter nights, he scans the sky
for Orion's three-starred belt, remembering
whose arms warmed him, the cold night
he first saw it; who told him its name.

Comfort

John Thomson, d. 1618

You would have to know where he lived,
how his croft clung to a hillside
forty times its size, on sufferance.

To stand under meteor showers
and northern lights, under a sky so vast
it swallowed his voice,

to see daily the breathtaking sweep
of hills, green and purple breakers
of surging stone,

to hear the ravishing inhuman voices
of birds, water, wind. You would need
to look out from his land,

where the ocean glitters beyond what eyes
can bear, the view he shared with no-one,
to understand John Thomson,

who, long ago, was strangled for seeking
the stable's warmth and, with soft words
of comfort, making love to his mare.

The Movement of Bodies

He fractured white light into seven colours,
reckoned the distance to the moon,

wrote laws for the movement
of bodies: no mystery to him

until now. Planets in their orbit,
the sea's tides, his eyes

locked to the lit face
of the young mathematician.

A body at rest remains so
unless some force act on it.

So many years, no joy
but in numbers, no troubling

of the flesh. The pink tongue-tip
idly licking a finger

constricts his heart. His edges
flicker, scintillate, like a heat-haze.

A hand brushes his cheek
and it colours: *to each action*

an equal and opposite reaction.
He tries to think straight:

the moon. I worked out its mass. Moonlight,
kissing in moonlight. The movement

of bodies. The moon draws
the tides. A knife in my eye.

Once, probing for truth,
he nearly blinded himself.

This time, he will flinch
from the lacerating light.

Legend will say he died a virgin
and never saw the sea.

The Gold Sky of Venus

When he was eight and book-mad, they took him
for the first time to a high building
full of books, furnished floor to ceiling
with shelves of songs, stories, answers, dreams,

and they said "choose", and he burst out crying,
because he knew that even in a lifetime
he'd never get to read all of them.
He can smile about it now. It's something

you get used to. What were once destinations
– Samarkand, Shanghai, Saqqara –
have become the places he never saw,
a slight ache in the imagination.

But tonight he watched a programme about Venus,
where sun never pierces the dense cloud
but glows behind it, turning it to gold,
and tonight the ache is worse, the sense of loss

and waste and unread books, and his life
that seems to him worth nothing if he must die
and never see the beaten-gold sky
of Venus, bearing down like pure grief.

Catnip

Deep inside, licking the pale-spiked bush,
stroking his tongue along the serrated edges

of minty leaves, setting free the scent
and rolling in it, over and over, breathing it

until his whole world is this piercing note
he can hardly hold, a psychosexual high

that sends him skittering, pawing at air,
glassy-eyed, mewing, breathing hard

and fast, till he falls asleep, complete
and exhausted. Hundreds of years ago,

so they say, hangmen chewed this root
before the job, before the careful positioning

of their man, before the sudden jerk
arched his body, before he collapsed limp.

You, my small mutated tiger, chew leaves
for fun only. When you want to kill,

you do it cold sober; you don't ask
the sparrow's forgiveness, and you don't pray.

The Navigator Loses the Sea

William Dampier, 1652–1715

Thirty years ago, he wrote the book
of these seas: two hundred years later,

they'll still be using it. Now he sails
as pilot to Woodes Rogers, back on the roads

and channels he once charted, an old man
looking out from the rail, and nothing he sees

is at all familiar. He can't find
the safe route to Juan Fernandez;

he's misplaced the Galapagos. They ask
about Butung. *No, I was never there.*

Later, below, he finds it in his book;
he spends a lot of time learning the names

and places that have slipped from his mind,
hoping to bluff the captain a bit longer.

A navigator who has lost the sea.
In the Cape Verdes, he reads of salt pans,

vast and silver, and his own excitement
at the great birds, more than he could count,

wherever he looked. "They were like a wall
of new red brick." He stares at the word,

its arbitrary, meaningless letters,
wondering what flamingos look like.

Stalemate

Carl Schlechter, 1874-1918

I want to stroll with Carl Schlechter
in nineteen-hundred, down a street of stone

the sun's turned to honey. From some window
a piano's playing slow, and Carl's sad eyes

kindle a little. I ask about his chess,
why he always offers a draw,

and he shrugs. White pigeons gurr
on the sills. "I hate that look in men's eyes

when they lose." I love him. We buy cherries
from a stall, morellos, dark, half-bitter,

and feed them to each other. I kiss him,
tasting them in his mouth. I want to tell him

"Carl, you die starving, at forty-four,
and you could be world champion. Play to win."

But then he wouldn't be who he is,
and I wouldn't come all the way

from the next century to hold hands
with the drawing master, watching

the light slant, hearing pigeons hush,
one by one, into sleep. Gentleman; gentle man.

The Bereavement of the Lion-Keeper

for Sheraq Omar

Who stayed, long after his pay stopped,
in the zoo with no visitors,
just keepers and captives, moth-eaten,
growing old together.

Who begged for meat in the market-place
as times grew hungrier,
and cut it up small to feed him,
since his teeth were gone.

Who could stroke his head, who knew
how it felt to plunge fingers
into rough glowing fur, who has heard
the deepest purr in the world.

Who curled close to him, wrapped in his warmth,
his pungent scent, as the bombs fell,
who has seen him asleep so often,
but never like this.

Who knew that elderly lions
were not immortal, that it was bound
to happen, that he died peacefully,
in the course of nature,

but who knows no way to let go
of love, to walk out of sunlight,
to be an old man in a city
without a lion.

Golden Rabbits

He came up for the peace, the scenery,
the stepping back in time, but mostly
because someone told him the rabbits here
were golden. At the time, he'd never
seen rabbits, and if he had, in truth,
they'd have been psychedelic, the stuff
he was on. But somehow the vision
stuck long enough to get him on a train,

a ferry, a bus, out to the far end
of a peninsula. The crofters were kind,
but they all laid bets he wouldn't last.
Around that time, a lot of folk lost
in the twentieth century took this road,
looking for peace, the truth, themselves, God.
Whatever they'd mislaid, the first storm
saw them give up on it and head for home.

But he's still here, after so long, growing
enough to get by, writing a bit, doing
small driving jobs. "You can't eat scenery",
someone said, but he can, very nearly.
The red rocks nightly catching fire,
a pod of whales, the odd meteor shower,
are what sustains him, like the peat stack
in his shed, or the big winter sack

of tatties. Most of the rabbits are brown,
same as anywhere, but just the odd one
isn't. His only road blocked by snow
each new year, he scrapes ice from his window
and watches them edge close to his scatterings
of crusts, carrot tops, potato peelings,
his heart stopping when, against the white,
one shape glows like clear honey in sunlight.

The Windfarm Angels

I'll never forget my first sighting:
one alone, on a distant hill
– they prefer hills. There was no wind
that day, none at all, and it stood
quite still. Its top arm, pointing
at the sky, blended into its body:
it was just this tall streak of white.
The two other arms stretched out
left and right, like the statue of Christ
in Rio harbour. That was how I knew
it was an angel. That, and the calm
that came off it. It didn't speak
or make a move: it just *was*,
intensely, and I felt better for it,
which is what they do, right?

After that, I looked out for them,
that sudden grace on the skyline,
whenever there seemed no point
in anything. One windy day, watching
a group of three, I realised they were talking,
not just in gesture language, but a murmur,
low, on one note. I couldn't tell
if they meant it only for each other
or for me too. I heard it in my head
long after. I'd switch off from chat,
traffic, muzak, and it was there.

I've noticed, lately, they don't talk
so loud. Even watching a whole flock,
I have to strain to hear. Folk complained
– would you believe – about the noise,
so now they whisper. And some people
want them gone. I couldn't face that,
not now. I've got used to that presence,
that white embrace, being there
when I need it. I know all their haunts.
To think I might climb those hills one day
and find them empty. Jesus.

Pride

He wears his age well, they say:
it's the silver hair, the straight back,

the fifty-year marriage, even.
But it isn't. The pride

inscribed in his eyes, his voice,
his quiet, private smile,

was burned into him decades back
by a kiss in a tent.

Close up, the glacier was fissured,
black with the dusty scribble

of hail and wind, but distance
perfected its whiteness. He lay

in the summer night of the north,
a blue half-dark

of whispered courtship, and fell
asleep on the numbed arm

of love. And next day,
love was frantic, scrabbling for paper

to write it all down. It was read to him,
softly; the others weren't looking,

and he wondered why the poem
was saying goodbye. One night?

He was at an age when the tune,
the summer, the fairground ride,

are always better repeated.
The secret, warm memory

of kisses could not console him
for the absence of kisses.

He thinks differently now. So far
from that time, he can see the problem:

he *was* sixteen, and the man
was the English master... And anyway,

the poem still shines, an ice-field
of unblemished love no weather

or time can write on, a landmark
of its century. Now, in his eighties,

he speaks it from memory, marvelling.
That was me? But it was. The knowledge

superb in his eyes, that hold
no more self-doubt than a hawk's.

Best Jesus in Show

See, these country shows, there's always classes
with maybe just one entry. *Six Jam Tarts
Baked by a Gentleman,* or *Female Goat
Not in Milk.* Well, the Jesus van
was like that. Every year, this Malcolm
shows up, in a camper with JESUS SAVES
on the side, parks by the tractors
and waits for people to come and pray.

Only this year, there's another one,
Society for Christian Somethingorother,
facing Malcolm across the show field.
Competition! And we're wondering how
to judge them. With sheep or needlework
or vegetables, there's criteria:
so many marks for size, presentation,
lack of blemishes... But then with tups
or turnips, you know how they're meant to look.

All we had to go on was Malcolm,
who's the hairy sort with sandals,
and this other bloke, who's a suit
and probably works in a call centre.
They're no more alike than a Limousin
and a Friesian, but somehow one of them
has to end up as Best Jesus in Show,
with the other as reserve champion.

Watching the folk group, someone suggested
banjos at noon. Duelling Jesuses?
Give them each five buns and some crackling
from the pig roast, and see which can feed
five thousand? The log-sawing contest
seemed possible, but they didn't fancy
raising a hand and telling the logs to part.

You couldn't use audience figures: no one
went near either of them. In the end
we didn't feel sure enough. Anyway,
there was only one spare rosette
in the committee tent, and the girls
nabbed that, wrote *Prettiest Policeman in Show*
on the ribbon, and gave it to the traffic plod
by the main gate.

The Grave of the Grande Armée at Vilnius

He must have been young indeed,
when he left his home in France,
or Poland, or Portugal,

to follow the Grande Armée.
Maybe he played a drum,
laughed up at the bearded faces,

kept time as they sang their way
over half a continent.
Only free men are men.

At Vilnius-on-two-rivers
they gathered, as summer came on,
and when the emperor said,

"Moscow in twenty days,"
maybe he cheered with the rest.
The sun rang, hammer on metal,

and they sang *Our Fan likes a drink*,
and the country sucked them in.
Week after week, they marched

into empty villages, fields
bare of crops, no one to fight,
only, around their edges,

kazakhs, the shadows of wolves,
swerving in, snapping, retreating.
The army started to fray,

slipping off, but he was still there,
singing *All the kings must weep*,
when they came to Borodino.

He did not die on the field,
where the fifty thousand were left
to stiffen in autumn frost.

He was with the Grande Armée
entering Moscow, the streets
uncanny and silent. Maybe

he saw a bit of the city,
before its hidden people
set it alight and ran.

Maybe he saw the emperor
ride past that wall of fire
that lit the tears on his face.

Maybe they did still sing
When all the tyrants are dead,
as they tramped the road they had come,

past the dead of Borodino,
past blackened house and field.
November, the first snow fell,

and they huddled close at night,
listening to the wolves.
They started to dream of food.

Fan was baptised in wine,
he'd sing, the rusty taste
of horse-blood still in his mouth.

They could not cling close enough
to keep out the frost; maybe
he lost an ear or a finger,

but he crossed the crazy pontoon
at the Beresina River.
A hundred were swept away,

but when the last of the army
lay starving outside Vilnius,
he was still there, still singing

We're all from the same country,
as the emperor slipped off for France.
Maybe he watched him go.

One grave for the bones of young men
from every land in Europe.
He had no wound: his body,

aching for warmth, was curled
the way, fifteen years before,
it had lain in his mother.

Adzio's Story

Adzio on the beach; he's eleven,
like the century, on holiday,

and the Adriatic is that blue he'll recall,
but never see again. He arches

like a cat, to make the sun stroke him,
warm, content. If he sees, for a moment,

on the edge of his vision, the old man
watching him again, it casts no shadow;

might just rate a mention in the diary,
if nothing more interesting turns up.

When he's grown, when he's Baron Moes
and no-one calls him Adzio any more,

he'll read the book, see the golden boy
and the dark, arm in arm, and know

– how slowly? – It's *me… me and Jasio.*
How will it feel, to watch himself played

like a chess piece, altered to fit
the story? *I wasn't fourteen,*

and why has he made me anaemic?
Looking back, he will think he recalls

eyes bright with hunger. *Only thirty-six?*
He seemed so old… The story shapes itself

to a new shoreline. *Did I fight Jasio?*
The horizon where what was real

shades into fancy is so far off,
so blurred, he can't make it out.

He will never come forward while the writer
still lives, never say *That was me*

you wrote about. The old man smiled to think
the boy would die young... It seems tactless

to stand, middle-aged, where the memory
of *him* should be. Adzio grew up,

but the boy with the honey-coloured hair
and the grey eyes has never left Venice;

still stands between sea and land, looking back
at the real, beckoning into the story.

Fiction

Camp 60, Orkney, 1945

It isn't a prison camp, if we plant flowers,
and this can't be the far north,
or why would we bring tables and chairs
outside, to dine alfresco? Our theatre
has proper scenery.

And this isn't a Nissen hut; do you see
corrugated iron anywhere? The brickwork
and the carved stone are only plasterboard
if you touch them. Take them with the eye;
believe what you see.

Chiocchetti is brilliant at painting shadows.
Look at the stone pillars, the gilded beams
of the vault; you can see they're solid.
If your fingers tell you different, will it change
what your eyes know?

Things become more than themselves.
Shipwreck wood is a tabernacle, scrap-iron
a rood screen. Those light-holders, hanging
from chains of silver stars, were beaten
out of tin cans.

Palumbo and Primavera shaped scrap
into candelabra; the white altar
is Bruttapasta's concrete, like the façade
with its belfry and pinnacles. You'd say
it was all marble,

because it seems a place where marble
should be, and sometimes what seems
is what is real. The font is concrete too,
but it looks like stone. Chiocchetti
is painting it

to seem weathered. I said, Domenico,
who gets christened, in a prison camp?
He didn't answer. The war is over,
we're all going home soon,
but he has asked

to stay, to finish work on a font
that isn't needed, in a chapel
whose congregation has left. It's gone
beyond him; you can see he's become
part of its story.

He worries about what will happen
to his creation, his face as haunted
as Pennisi's clay Christ above the door.
All we needed was a Nissen hut,
somewhere to call

a chapel. Our theatre has real scenery,
but nothing to match the gold curtains
of our vestry, that open for a man
of earth to step through, transfigured
into a priest.

The Street of Small Houses

Wooden booths, just big enough for one,
leaned close on a street stifled

with caraway, saffron, aniseed.
The old men pattered out on their errands

for food and firewood in the peppery air,
sneezing. They were foreigners, clerks

to the spice merchants, settled
among strangers who slowly turned

into neighbours. They went shopping
for small amounts. The city forbade them

marriage: they might live
and trade, but leave no mark.

On the Street of Small Houses
windows were paned

with horn or skin: scant outlook
for the old bachelors.

They got handy about the house,
used to long silences,

fond of their own company. They grew
apart from each other, lost their language

for one in which they would never
take vows or christen children.

They aged into habits, teased by the songs
of boys. Their walks grew shorter

and they passed fewer men they knew
to nod to in the street where ginger

had lost its bite. They drew their houses
round them like dressing-gowns.

Buying Vinyl

I was asking Cal about floor coverings
– I knew it was Cal because his cardboard badge

said CAL in black felt-tip. What I needed
was six metres of wood-effect vinyl

on a roll, and a good reason to fix
Cal's eyes with mine for a few moments

while I told him about it. They were brown,
far darker than the vinyl, forest-pool-effect.

I showed him what I wanted, and he nodded
and said "yes, right away" and spread

the stuff out on the floor and knelt down.
The back of his neck looked as untouched

as new snow. He glanced up under his eyebrows,
shy, and said, "Do me a favour,

hold this still?" So I did, kneeling
beside him at the edge, pressing my hand

where his had been, while he laid
his long steel rule close to the roll

and cut. Clean, straight, beautiful.
I said, "You're good at that" and he smiled,

and I thought, *You can't be more than seventeen.*
He rolled it tight, not easy, the tip

of his tongue just showing, and I wanted
to help, but he hadn't asked, and I was meant

to be the customer, after all.
I'm three times your age. And he mastered it.

All tied up firmly. I was proud of him.
He puzzled for a moment, licked

the end of his biro, then wrote the bill.
"You pay them over there." It was good value,

I thought, as I checked the VAT,
and he hadn't even charged for the smile.

In Love Without

Being *in love with* would be easy,
together in that place where no path
leads where it ought, in that curious light
where perspective goes all to hell.
The two moons, the Escher staircases,
the clueless maze, they'd be pure adventure
if they were mirrored in your eyes
and his; if he were there with you.

But you're in love without, seeing aslant
what he sees straight, lost on the roads
that take him home. It's another country
in the same space, in no eyes but yours.
Close by, far off, he laughs; waves a hand
past your face. "What planet are you on?"

The Thief of Love

I will come like a thief if I have to,
soft-footed. I won't force an entry,
just find one,

some sash with a gap. I'll slip
a fingertip in, ease it open
while you're asleep.

You'll be out when I feel your cool sheets
on my skin, when I stroll through your rooms
handling, enjoying.

I'll access your email, your passwords,
click on your history, trace you
through cyberspace.

Did you think I would come to the door
as honest folk do, play fair?
Love has no pride,

no honour; it takes what it's given
and what it can get. It begs
without shame: why not this?

And I am each chancer, levanter
and picklock who gives his heart freely
to what's out of reach,

far above, safely owned, and schemes how
to coax it to hand, one way
or another.

Love Is

Each time you go out, I wonder
if you'll meet them, the ones
warped beyond help,

bored enough to break
what can be broken:
benches, saplings, bones.

Love is knowing they're out there
even when they aren't.

I see their smiles
as they call you. I see
your face, open,

trusting, as they take you
to some unwatched place.
I see your eyes

widen as they turn
on you, and I think
they laugh, then,

at your pain, but still more
at your surprise; how easy
it was to fool you.

Love is dreaming things they could do
that even they don't guess.

Up to the moment
when you walk through the door
whole, smiling, safe,

you are lying in the dark
I made in my head,
and their grins are fixed

where my blade etched them.
Your name, which they never
cared to ask,

I burn carefully,
with a flourish of pokerwork,
into their flesh.

Love is knowing I could do
anything they could.

Ballad of the Lovesick Traveller

You roll a rizla, and your friends
half-heartedly protest,
but she, ex-smoker that she is,
lights it and holds your wrist.
We fan the acrid smoke away,
she tastes it in your kiss.
And what is that but love, my dear,
when nothing tastes amiss?

She's twenty-five; she wants to dance
and feel the pulsing sound.
You're fifty-four; you smile and shrug
and let her take your hand.
On each young face you read the words
No fool like an old fool.
And what is that but love, my dear,
that doesn't mind at all?

She counts the days like miracles
since all the world was new.
You see your image in her eyes
and can't believe it's you.
We, on the edge of all that light,
feel opened, warmed, alive.
And what is that but love, my dear,
that has so much to give?

You crossed the world to see old friends,
not thinking any harm.
Now all your journeys lead elsewhere
and nothing is the same.
And in your home of thirty years,
the one whose trust you have
expects you like tomorrow's post.
And what is that but love?

The Ex-Poet Writes HTML

He types "go here"; encloses it
in an anchor ref. Now, if you click
on the words,

the thing will happen. He writes code
to make words dance, change colour,
come alive.

He can make them shape the image
of his new book cover,
with secret text

embedded; when the cursor rests,
adventure leaps out.
And he can't believe

the power, the way words move,
at last, as he wants,
the way they turn

into sounds and patterns, the way
they send his readers
on the journey

he chose for them. He spends
whole days online, can't sleep
for thinking up

page after page, hooked
on creation, and he hasn't written
a poem in months.

Flying Into Sunset

He's flying late, above dense cloud,
close-coiled rope on a ship's deck,

toward the core of all redness
bleeding rose, wine, molten copper

over the blue-white ice-field, and nobody
watching below the cloud, he knows,

ever saw these colours. They'll be going
home now, the earthbound,

escaping from work. Little clumps
of pink cumulus like tumbleweed

blow across the flight path. And they pay him
to do this, to be here, though he knows

he'd pay them. And when the blaze
narrows to a red line, goes out,

all the matches at once, it leaves no dark,
not up here, just uncanny blue,

perpetual day, a story
with no last line, a childhood

out of time. *No-one saw where
the bird went, but some said it flew*

straight into the sun. In the ice-field
polynyas open: he can see the dark,

ocean-deep, below him, trembling
with threaded points of light,

and it's Birmingham, but he doesn't need
to know that yet.

Learning Hindi

I rolled an incorrect r
and my life took a new peacock.

Words misprint as worlds
all the time. I woke

with a new voice, raucous
and haunting. Though I walked

in the old way, eyes
bent on the ground, my humility

was only manners.
In my mind there hid,

folded, the northern lights,
a curtain waterfall

of colours, trembling
like jewels on thin wire.

Almost blue, almost green, almost purple,
too iridescent

to pin down, vibrations
in the air, eye-music.

I can hear the notes, unplayed,
I don't need to open

the great, rustling sheaf.
So heavy, so secret,

what I am. Only
my cry, shaking,

ragged with delight,
gives me away.

The Curious Drawer

How then can the curious drawer watch, and as it were catch those lovely graces, witty smilings and those stolen glances which suddenly like lightning pass, and another countenance taketh place?
— Nicholas Hilliard: *The Arte of Limning*

1. The Ermine

And with a pretty little tooth of some ferret or stoat or other wild little beast you may burnish your gold and silver.

She is almost lost in points of light.
Her gown the dark ground, sown

with gold and silver, stiff with jewels,
her ruff a radiance, as if

her face shed moonlight. I have made
filigree of her hair. On her left sleeve,

through intricate patterns, crevasses
of velvet, a small wild creature

climbs like a pet. You may see,
if you will, majesty

in the tiny crown it wears, virginity
in the startling white I ground

on jasper and mixed in a clean shell.
I see suddenness, unsuspected

ivory daggers, a swift savagery
that takes the breath away.

2. Young Man Among Roses

Know also that parchment is the only good
and best thing to limn on, but it must be
virgin parchment, such as never bore hair,
but young things found in the dam's belly

I lean him against my wall,
which I will turn
into an oak,

his head inclining
to its rough bark
as if he listened

to some friend. Too slender
his long legs, like some deer
or colt half-grown.

I hang his cloak
off one shoulder,
feigning negligence,

lay his right hand
above his heart,
as who should say

'I am in love',
then I make roses
grow all around him,

pattern the ground
of his white hose
with their airy stems.

On the black cloak
pale buds, picked out
like pearls. Roses arch

over him, curve him
to the trunk where his sorrows
would like to seek

shelter, where he would curl,
if it were hollow,
rocking in the dark.

3. Sidney's Sister

The best black is velvet black,
which is ivory burnt in a crucible

Is it not strange that bone
should burn black?

Ashes sealed from the air
in salted clay,

fired red-hot, then cooled,
softened with water,

drop by drop, for her gown.
Within a perfect circle

I nest circles, white ruff
on black velvet,

red curls against a sky
of ultramarine, jet beads

clasping a white throat
close. Circles of lace,

hair, stone, drawing the gaze
inward to the stillness

at the heart
of all the circles,

her frozen face,
her bereaved eyes.

4. Henry Percy, 9th Earl of Northumberland

I would wish anybody to be well resolved
with themselves beforehand with what grace
they would stand, and seem as though they
never had resolved

Pansies and violets, petals
bruised and soaked, gave me green,

the lawn he lay on
in his black suit. Some scholar

or divine he seemed
among the flowers, even

with that wave of lace breaking
at collar and cuff.

His hair, brown–gold, combed back
softly, his cheek resting

on one white hand, his body
stretched out at ease.

The book, pink–tasselled,
forgotten at his elbow,

fallen open at love poems
perhaps, or the holy psalms,

anywhere but the history
of his rebel kin,

plotters, traitors, kingmakers
whose blood bloomed

on the scaffold, in the Tower
and across the fields

of Shrewsbury, Towton, Bramham Moor,
drenching the grass.

5. Unknown Young Man against
a Background of Flames

Let your apparel be of silk, such as
sheddeth least dust or hairs

My sitters come dressed in their finest: it is I
who must stand bare-headed before them
in a plain white shirt. My colours
are fresh-mixed in the shell, water distilled,
gum arabic pure in its ivory box.
On the burnished card where a face will live
for ever, nothing of me must fall,
not a hair nor a fleck of dandruff. I curb
my tongue, for fear of spittle. In cold weather
I breathe behind my hand.

I am skilled in surfaces: the depth of velvet,
the dazzle of lace, the way light wells
from a pearl or scatters off diamond. But here
is undress, flesh glowing
through thin silk, more ardent
than the flames of love, or so
he would have someone think. He fondles
the chain against his bare throat, shows
the ring on his hand: see, I wear
your tokens. I burn for you.

This penitent in silk, this martyr
to love. When you hold him
close in his jewelled case, remember
limning is an art of secrets. I look
for a face few have seen. That longing
in his eyes, he was gazing
at his warm cloak, hung
carefully on my wall,
while I opened his thin shirt,
the match of mine.